Life...

It's As Good
As You Make It

Life...
It's As Good
As You Make It

RON WOODS

Bookcraft
Salt Lake City, Utah

Incidents and portrayals in this book are fictitious

Library of Congress Catalog Card Number: 90–83213
ISBN 0–88494–763–7

First Printing, 1990

Printed in the United States of America

To Linda and Debbie

Contents

Preface

I didn't know life would be this way." This was the statement made, a few years ago, by a friend facing a crisis. Most of us can probably identify with her feelings. As we advance through life, all of us come up against realities that differ in some ways, large or small, from the ideals we had envisioned. At these difficult times we can find ourselves asking questions like these:

"How did I get into this situation?"

"Is this how I want things to be?"

"Where do I fit into the scheme of things, the big picture?"

"Is there anything I can do about how things are going or am I merely a pawn being swept along by forces beyond my control?"

"Who am I really? Who have I become? Who do I want to be?"

These are big questions with big answers, and the answers vary with each person. Further, the answers change for each of us as we go through life. Our answers at twenty-five will have changed by thirty-five and again by forty-five, fifty-five, sixty-five, and seventy-five.

We all respond to greater or lesser degrees to forces outside us. At work, at church, and in society at large, expectations are placed on us. These forces and expectations are not necessarily bad, but they each carry a price—which is that we may come to feel we are not making our own choices.

In explaining unhappiness, failures, and poor behavior, we tend to blame our environment. But as James Allen said, "Good thoughts bear good fruit, bad thoughts bear bad fruit—and man is his own gardener."

In contrast, in our culture people often say, "I couldn't help myself." People use this pathetic phrase to explain away fits of violent temper, addictions of all kinds, and even marital infidelity! While there may be individuals with psychological or physiological defects that make self-control more difficult or perhaps impossible, these are surely rare. Most of us can control what we wish to control.

Poor behaviors are learned behaviors. They can be un-learned. Put me in a frustrating situation in a room full of people who, consciously or not, and perhaps through sym-pathy, reward me for poor behavior, and I may feel that the situation "makes" me vent my frustration in unseemly ways. However, put me in the same frustrating situation in the middle of a room full of sleeping tigers (seldom known for their rewards or their sympathy), and I will probably act differently. In the latter case I may decide rather quickly not to let my frustration cause me to "act out." Somehow I manage to decide to control myself—proving I am actually in charge all along, when I want to be.

Therefore, the question of control is the central one for this book: How much say do I have about the person I am and will be?

And the answer is: A great deal.

The Lord has told us, "For behold, ye are free; ye are permitted to act for yourselves; for behold, God hath given unto you a knowledge and he hath made you free." (Hel. 14:30.) He expects us to make the choices that set the course for our own lives.

Of course, we can't do everything. There will be events outside our control—many, many of them. Crises will come, problems arise, disappointments and setbacks oc-cur. These can be counted on; no person who lives to maturity will escape them! Sooner or later life delivers a share of fear and uncertainty to each of us.

However, that doesn't absolve us of the responsibility to make choices and provide the principal guidance and direction for our own lives. The concept of accountability remains clear and unassailable: The responsibility for the happiness and the success of my life still rests with me, yours with you.

As we reach those occasional, inevitable awakenings in life when our souls are bared and the need for self-renewal is realized, we face a difficult choice. That choice is whether to follow our higher instincts toward progression and joy or to follow the inclinations of the "natural man" toward stagnation and defeat.

If we choose progression, we choose the higher, steeper, harder—but better—road. Breaking loose from the past and taking greater control of the future are seldom as easy, at least in the short run, as sitting back and accepting whatever life offers. But the purpose of our existence is not to fill our easy chairs but to fulfill our destinies.

Our stewardship for self is, therefore, a most important one, even a divine one. A concern with self need not be selfish or self-centered. On the contrary, through looking at where we have been, where we are and where we are going, we become partners with God in our own creation.

In this book short vignettes are used to portray adults of all ages and stations in life encountering questions of who they are and who they will be. You will see them handle these challenges with varying degrees of understanding, courage, and success. As you read these stories you will undoubtedly identify with many of them, because they deal with common concerns which most of us face, in one form or another, at some point in our lives. These examples may help you clarify choices in your own vital, ongoing efforts at self-design and self-improvement. Life really is as good as you make it.

1

Regrets: Dealing with the Past

Occasionally a person will say, "If I had my life to live over again, I wouldn't change a thing." This has always seemed a rather shallow and untenable viewpoint. Surely all of us have at least a few regrets about immature choices made, cruel words uttered, and opportunities bypassed. Surely, if we could go back, at the least we would want to avoid the poison ivy, the parking tickets, and the sunburns! Saying we wouldn't change a thing implies we've learned nothing from our experiences.

But the question is moot—we cannot live our lives again. Isabel Moore says, "Life is a one-way street. No matter how many detours you take, none of them leads back." Of the three divisions of time—past, present, future—the past is the only one we can do nothing about. Nothing, that is, except what is sometimes the hardest thing of all: accept it. For some people, acceptance is a terribly difficult thing. They are the opposite of those who would change nothing; they would change what can't be changed.

The past is vital to our understanding of ourselves, the basis for our existence in the present. Our past, and our memories of it, make us who we are. But as Jan Glidwell says, "You can clutch the past so tightly to your chest that it leaves your arms too full to embrace the present." Making peace with the past isn't always easy, but it's always necessary, if we're to have happiness in the present. Inevitably, we must learn to say goodbye, let go, adjust—as people in the following vignettes have done, are doing, or should do.

Failed Dreams or Adjusted Dreams?

"Grandpa, can I see your clippings book?"

"Why, sure, Lane. An old hoofer like me is always glad to show off his pictures. Get it out of the bedroom, will you? Ten-year-old legs work better than eighty-two-year-old ones."

"What's a hoofer, Grandpa?"

"Get the book and I'll show you."

By the time Lane came back with a fat binder bulging with photos and newspaper clippings, his grandfather was seated at the dining room table. "Put it right here, Lane, on the table." He opened to a page near the front and pointed to an old picture of a much-younger Leo Rudolph in top hat and tuxedo, complete with cane and white, silk scarf. "That, my boy, is a hoofer."

"You mean somebody dressed up like that?"

"No, boy, look at my feet—virtually floating."

"Is that you, Grandpa? Are you dancing?"

"Now you've got it! A hoofer is a dancer. I'll bet you didn't know I was a dancer, did you? Actually, I didn't do much with it after I got my start. Most of my stage work didn't involve dancing, but you had to know the basics in those days. Let's look through, and you'll see."

"Okay."

"Have you ever seen these before, Lane?"

"A long time ago, when I was little. Mom told me when I came to stay this time to be sure and have you show me."

"Glad to do it, Son. Your mom used to look through these same pictures when she was your size, but they weren't in a nice book like this. Your grandma organized all these, a few years before she died. So, let's go. These first pages show the different revues I was in, starting even before I met your grandma."

"Your hair was black?"

"Oh, sure, black as the night. Darker than yours, I'll bet."

"You looked young, Grandpa."

Leo laughed. "We're all young once, Lane. Eighteen in that one." He pointed to a yellowed cast picture. "My very first show—1926. Minneapolis. It closed in four days— about three too late."

Together they looked through the pages. Lane asked questions and Leo gave answers. At one point Lane asked, "Who's this, Grandpa? She's pretty."

"Three guesses, big boy," Leo said.

"It must be Grandma."

"Sure is. I met her when I worked a radio series in St. Paul. See that old-fashioned microphone in front of us?"

"Were you on TV, Grandpa?"

"Ha! No such thing in those days."

"Really?"

Leo laughed. "The St. Paul days were great days, Lane. We were going to set the world on fire, we were."

"What do you mean?" Lane asked.

"Why, your grandma and I were determined we would make it big, go on to Hollywood or New York—be rich, be famous, be stars!"

"You must have been famous, with all these pictures."

"No, son, I wasn't famous. Never quite made it. We were coming along pretty well, though, keeping busy, surviving. And then times got tough, theaters shut their doors, the depression closed in, war came. And the family had started coming along—your uncle Hank, Aunt Sue, your mom. Somehow we kind of let go of that dream and went on to others. I decided to go back to college, and ended up teaching."

"I read a book about a woman who wanted to be a star, and when she couldn't she had a bunch of divorces and stuff, and she never was happy," Lane said.

"Well, that's an interesting thing, Lane. There were times when I felt that maybe we should have stuck with it a little longer, like I'd failed. I'd done so much bragging about what I was going to do." Leo shook his head and smiled ruefully. "But I didn't spend a lot of time feeling sorry for myself. Your grandma wouldn't tolerate that! And we sure didn't get any divorces and stuff!

"Sometimes, when we'd hear from friends who'd stayed with the stage and made a go of it, I'd get a little down. She knew what was wrong—she always did, that woman—and she'd say, 'Leo, think of what you have, not what you don't have.'

"And I had a lot. The pleasure I found in teaching drama and directing college productions—it was good. So, no, Lane, I may not have been famous, but I don't have any regrets anymore. My dreams did come true, after all, even though they changed a little first. And who knows, if I hadn't aimed for a stage career, I'd have never made it to where I had the most ability—teaching.

"Besides, like Grandma used to say, 'If none of your dreams fail, you didn't have enough to start with.' "

Leo appears to have had some struggles letting go of his dream. And that's understandable. Dreams are nothing more or less than strongly desired goals, and they necessarily have a powerful hold on us. They *shouldn't* be given up easily. But they can be changed or adjusted, and sometimes they must be. It is fortunate that our happiness depends more on our ability to adjust our dreams than on our ability to accomplish our original ones.

We praise and admire those we occasionally hear of who, after years of effort, finally accomplish exactly what they set out to do—win a competition, attain a college degree, fly an airplane. But we seldom hear of others who hold on for too long.

The fact is that some of the most unhappy people in the world are those who cling to dreams that simply cannot come to pass. Or that cannot do so without doing violence to other ideals. Such people need a dream adjustment! It's wonderful and exciting and fulfilling to sell the house and quit the job in order to buy a yacht and sail around the world—as long as it doesn't leave behind the wreckage of a family without a home or means of support!

Leo has adjusted well to his failed dreams. Which of his present blessings would he trade away to be able to go back and "set the world on fire"?

Righting Old Wrongs: It's Never Too Late

Professor Puckett came back to his office after class, put down his books and notes, and sat down. As he opened his drawer to get his brown-bag sandwich, he glanced through the mail the department secretary had put on his desk.

There was the usual assortment of campus flyers and lecture announcements, a notice of an upcoming faculty meeting, an invitation to a retirement reception for a colleague, an always-welcome monthly salary check. And an envelope, hand-addressed, with a postmark from three states away. On both the front and the back was printed "PERSONAL."

Probably a former student wanting a job recommendation, he thought as he slit open the envelope.

"Dear Professor Puckett," the letter began. "You won't remember me." He leaned back to read. "I was in your general education Biology 320 class years back."

Good grief, 320! Dr. Puckett thought as he recognized the old course numbering system that had been replaced in the early 1970s.

He read on: "I think it was 1970 or '71. Well, here's the problem. I got a 'B' in your class, but I cheated on the final exam to do it."

"Uh-oh!" Dr. Puckett breathed aloud. He put down his half-eaten sandwich.

"I'm sorry to be so long in confessing and I'm sorry to bother you with this problem, but it has been gnawing on me for a long time. I'm ashamed and appalled that I could have done what I did. I certainly have no excuse. Here are the facts, for you to decide what to do.

"I was in a morning section, in the fall semester, although I can't remember which year. It couldn't have been later than 1971, though, because I graduated in the spring of 1972."

Professor Puckett realized that the details really had little to do with the problem but that they seemed to be a necessary part of the confession process for most people. His heart went out to the writer, whose name at the bottom of the page he did not recognize after so many years.

"I feel doubly bad, Professor Puckett, because I not only cheated on the exam, but I lied about it to your face.

"You see, we were taking the exam and you left the room for a time. I purposely sat near the back, and as soon as you were gone I slipped out of my pocket some notes I'd prepared on a small slip of paper. These helped me with several of the answers. I was just finishing with the notes when I looked up to see a girl two rows over looking right at me. She continued to stare, and I knew for sure that she saw what I was doing.

"I didn't know what to do, so I just went on with the test and made sure I left before the girl did. That afternoon you called me and asked me to come to your office. Of course, I knew what you wanted. I tried to make myself feel better by hating the girl for telling on me, but in my heart I knew she wasn't the problem—I was. I agonized over what to do because I had a job waiting for me in the spring and I *had* to graduate on time.

"By the time I got to your office, I had rationalized that even without my cheat sheet I would have passed the test. I knew I'd done the wrong thing, but I couldn't bring myself to face the music, which would have meant at the least re-taking the class, I figured. But my winter schedule was too tight, and I couldn't have graduated on time.

"So, when I met with you I feigned innocence and said I'd remembered a note my roommate had given me about calling someone for him. I said I had just thought of that note and had pulled it out of my pocket to make sure of the time, when the girl looked at me. I said I knew she thought I was cheating, but that since I wasn't, I didn't worry about what she thought. I gave quite an impassioned little per-formance about how people shouldn't judge others, and said that if she wanted to come and face me, I'd be glad to go get the note out of my wastebasket at home and show it to her.

"All of it was a bold-faced lie, of course, although I'd have carried it through and *created* a phony note if I'd had to. But you believed me, to your credit and my shame, and told me to never mind."

By this point Professor Puckett actually did vaguely remember such an incident, although no details were clear. It had boiled down to one person's word—and perhaps flawed observation—against another, and the accused young man had been so convincing that he had felt it not worth pursuing. Since it was unlikely that one slip of paper could have made the difference in a passing and a failing grade in the course, it had seemed best to drop the matter.

He read on. "I went out of there feeling very relieved— even justified. How ironic that even though I knew I would have passed the test without the notes, I felt compelled to use them.

"I can't tell you how much this has bothered me all these years. Since I had not cheated in other classes and only did so in this case because I had gotten behind and felt I had to do it, I kept feeling guilty, but justified. But now and then, when I've talked to my own children about honesty, or when I've taught church classes, or when I've heard my wife tell our kids to be honest 'like your dad is,' I've been nearly overwhelmed with guilt.

"I must get this settled. So I'm writing you to ask that you help me decide what must be done. If need be, I will return my diploma and do whatever else is necessary to clear up my past. I need to be free from this.

"Thank you very much. Sincerely, . . ."

There was a P.S. It read, "Thank you again. I'm starting to feel better already."

Exorcising the regrets of the past is like pulling out porcupine quills—removal can be a wrenching thing, probably only exceeded in pain by *not* exorcising them and leaving them there to fester still longer.

How painful writing this letter must have been, but what a relief sending it must have been! The writer has reached the point, however belatedly, of looking back at a past event and being able to say, with humility, disbelief, and repugnance, "How could I have done that?"

The next step is to be able to say, "I am no longer the same person who did that deed. I would not, could not, do such a thing now." This realization—this rebirth—is a major step of true repentance.

Few people enjoy a visit to the dentist. Yet, when compared to the pain of a toothache, the lesser pain of having a tooth filled is like a warm breeze in January. Just as the dentist sometimes has to inflict pain in order to make repairs, so is correcting errors from our past a painful but necessary part of the healing process. For in repairing our past, we're repairing ourselves. And it's never too late.

Memory—Don't Bet on It

"This thing is getting out of hand, folks," Raleigh chuckled. "You'd think with a group this size we could get some kind of consensus on something this simple. Do you or do you not remember where you were when you first heard of the Kennedy assassination? Raise your hands if you're absolutely certain you remember."

Every adult over thirty-five in the family reunion group raised a hand, as did three or four others who couldn't have been out of kindergarten in 1963.

Someone said, "How could anybody forget anything like that?"

"Now," Raleigh answered, "I'll lay you odds that if you were to talk with someone who was with you at the same moment you might find that your memory isn't what you think—even for these major events that we're all so sure we remember perfectly. Even these 'flashbulb memories,' as they're called, aren't very accurate. There have been studies. I've read about it."

"Well, I know how *I* heard it," Leola, Raleigh's older sister, said. "You called me yourself, and that's the first I heard of it."

"Oh?" Raleigh said. "That's interesting. Where did I call you from?"

"Now, don't try to trip me up, Raleigh. I'm your big sister. I don't remember all that. But I know you called and we talked about it."

"You're right that I called you, but I couldn't have been the first to tell you about it—not unless you lived in a cave. Because, if you'll recall, I was in the service at the time, and I happen to know that over the whole of that Thanksgiving weekend I was quarantined in a base hospital in the Philippines, while they figured out if the hives and splotches I'd developed were anything contagious. And there was no phone in that room, sister. I couldn't have called you until at least the next Monday when I got out."

"Well, I don't know," Leola said. "It's how I remember it."

Whichever of these two siblings has the facts straight in this case, Raleigh is right in his contention about memory. Studies show that our memories are remarkably inaccurate, even of events we're sure we'll never forget: Pearl Harbor, Kennedy's death, the Challenger explosion, the neighbor's house fire.

While it's true that *something* is vividly etched into our brains, that something may not be indisputable fact. It is probable that most of us have had the experience of clearly "recalling" a family incident that turned out to have happened before our birth! What we really remembered is the *imagined* scene resulting from hearing family members discuss the event. As they talk we "see" the event in our minds, and that imagined scene is what becomes our memory. Over time we're sure we were really there.

The morning after the space shuttle Challenger exploded in January of 1986 a researcher asked 100 college students to record how, where, and when they heard the news. Two-and-a-half years later, forty-four of the students were tracked down and interviewed. When their "indelible," flashbulb memories of the disaster were compared with their earlier on-the-spot responses, personally handwritten at the time, *none* of them was totally correct. In fact, eleven of the forty-four were completely wrong in *all* the pertinent facts.

There's another interesting twist to memory. One study indicates that people who have a positive view of themselves, as shown in psychological tests, actually have trouble recalling negative events. Their memories are selective, with a bias toward the positive.

We've realized for years that thinking positively about oneself can help create a self-fulfilling prophecy. Now we see that such positive thinking may also "create" a self-fulfilling *past!* (The opposite is presumed to be true, as well: those who see life negatively may remember mostly negative things and fail to recall the positive ones.)

It appears that the memory is a less effective recorder than it is a sorter, sifter, and editor. Perhaps that's why one folklorist suggests that our family histories are really not histories, but novels—stories built around themes and concepts and feelings and characters, more than around so-called *facts.*

Recognizing the limitations and biases of our memories can help us not only to be more humble and realistic about our "certainties" but also to better understand the people we have become. Through what kinds of eyes have you created your past—and, therefore, yourself?

Sometimes, All We Can Do Is Let It Be

Maxine was passing by the kitchen telephone when it rang. She picked it up before the first ring had ended.

"Maxine, how are you?" the voice on the other end said.

"Connie? Is that you?"

"Sure is. How are you doing?"

"We're all fine. How about you guys?"

"Fine here, too."

"Is Dad okay?"

"Yes, he's doing very well—considering."

"Considering what?"

"Well, that he's ninety-four. I think he's tolerating us pretty well, actually."

"Good. I'll admit," Maxine said, "that whenever you call my first thought is always that there might be something wrong."

"No, he's doing great. He's out raking leaves right now with a couple of the kids."

"Great," Maxine chuckled. "He does awfully well. When he was with us he fit right in and insisted on doing his share."

"There's one thing I want to ask you, though, while he's outside," Connie said. "How do I get him to write his life history? I've preached at him about it, even told him I'd take it down in shorthand or record it, if he would just talk. But I get no response whatsoever."

Maxine sighed and sat down at the table. "Let me tell you what's going on there, Connie. I've been through this before.

"I pushed him and pushed him on this after Mom died. Then, about fifteen years ago, something happened that I may never have mentioned to any of you. One day Dad got me in the car and we drove up to the foothills. He wouldn't tell me what we were doing until he got parked. Then he said, 'I want to talk with you about my history.' I thought, 'Oh, boy, he's finally going to do it.'

"Instead, he said, 'I'm going to tell you just enough to let you know why I'm never going to write it.' And then he told me things I never dreamed about his youth, about his treatment by . . . well, by others in his life—I see no reason to mention who they were. He wouldn't want me to." Maxine was crying now. "It was the saddest thing I've ever heard in my life, Connie. It broke my heart to hear my daddy telling me these things, and to learn why he couldn't write an honest—or even halfway honest—history without telling these things. He couldn't do it because these terrible things went on for years and affected everything he did for the first twenty years of his life and even caused him to get into a lot of trouble himself, until he turned his life around.

"He said he'd not even told Mom the full story, and he wasn't about to tell it to me. He cried like a baby and then he said, 'Maxine, these things are going to die with me. I decided that long ago. There is nothing to be learned by passing them on to future generations to read about. I can't do it. I won't do it. Don't ask me to do it.' "

Whether this man is correct that there's "nothing to be learned" by passing on his story, it's *his* life, and he can decide. I suspect that there are quite a few people unwilling to write their life histories because of painful childhoods. It seems reasonable that they should be allowed to make that decision.

In such a case, the children and grandchildren can still try to get them to describe the portions of their lives that they feel good in talking about. But a full, year-by-year description may be out of the question. If they can't bear a close look, let it be. A person has a right to be his own editor when it comes to abuse and other matters of gravity.

Sometimes the greatest gift such a person can give his posterity is to let the worst parts of his life history die with him.

Letting Go of the Pain

Roger Crowe left his classroom and went down the corridor to the main office. The corridors always seemed so different after the students had left for the day. The silence was almost eerie. He passed through the vacant front office and stepped up to the door marked Principal. The door was open and Joan Ritting sat at her desk.

"Dr. Ritting," Roger said.

"Yes, Roger, come in and sit down."

Roger complied.

"Dr. Ritting, huh?" Joan chuckled. "Pretty formal for old friends, isn't it?"

"Well, I guess I was a rowdy kid for enough years in school that I never will get over being a little intimidated when I'm called to the principal's office."

"I'm sure you're puzzled as to why I wanted to see you, and particularly at four o'clock."

"Well, I had plenty of paperwork to keep me here, so it's no problem," he said. But she was right; he was puzzled. It wasn't the standard time of day for a principal-teacher meeting.

"The reason I chose this time is so that we could talk for a few minutes without interruption."

"Oh. Okay," Roger said.

Joan stood up and came from behind her desk to sit in a chair next to his. "Roger, what I want to say to you today has nothing to do with the fact that I'm the principal. I hope I can talk to you as a friend."

"Oh, uh, sure," he said. What was she getting at?

"I've known you for a long time, and I know you like a direct approach to things, so I'm just going to come out with it. I can only apologize in advance if you feel that what I say is none of my business.

"Roger, you've been a teacher—a fine one—in this district for twenty years longer than I've been in education altogether. There is no teacher at this high school whom I respect more and value more as part of this team. I think you know that."

"Thank you," Roger said.

"But you're not doing well this year. You know it. I know it. Your students know it. Probably your wife and family and everybody else knows it. And we know why. And because we know why, nobody blames you—nobody at all. You have a lot of friends, Roger, and we all wish this terrible thing hadn't happened."

So that's it, Roger thought. Another well-meant attempt to make me feel better about the accident. He shifted uncomfortably.

Joan went on. "You're carrying a burden that nobody can carry for long, Roger, and it's going to wear you down if you don't throw it off. You've expressed to me and to others that you accept full responsibility for that student's death because you were in charge of the field trip last fall. Yet, you were cleared of blame. Everybody's tried to help you see that the student was negligent and went against the very rules you had set up, but it hasn't helped. You've taken upon yourself a guilt that is consuming you, ruining you as a teacher and as a person. Roger, it's a terrible enough tragedy already without making it worse by letting it destroy you, too."

"Nobody understands how it feels," Roger said quietly, his voice shaking. He looked down at his hands.

"Roger, I'm going to tell you something today that few people in this town know. I do it hoping it will help you. If it doesn't, I don't know what else to do. But I beg you to listen carefully.

"Nineteen years ago this month, before I'd gone back to school to get my doctorate and had moved to this state, I buried my first baby."

Roger looked up. Joan's voice grew a little husky, but she went on without a pause. "He was fourteen months old. I left him in the bathtub for a moment while I went to tune in a stupid radio show." She suddenly stood and turned away, facing the window.

"At the funeral they had to carry me out. At the graveside my husband and my father had to pull me off the casket so it could be lowered. They had to drag me to the car.

"Someone had made a tape, an audio tape, of the funeral, and I played it over and over and over—six, eight, ten times a day. As soon as my husband left for work I would turn on the tape. I would sit in the rocking chair where I had rocked my baby, in his room, and hold his blanket and toys and pictures, and I would play that tape until Carter came home. I would put it all away then, because I knew he would think I was insane. The trouble is, he would have been right." She turned back to face Roger, who was watching her intently.

Her voice was calm again now. "I wore that tape out, played it until there was nothing left to play, patched it with Scotch tape as often as I could, until it was finally in pieces. And then I would sit and recite the funeral to myself. I didn't need the tape anymore. I can probably quote every word of it still today."

She pointed a finger at Roger and her eyes were bright, but her voice quiet. "So don't you tell me that nobody knows how it feels."

Joan sat down again and went on. "One day, after

nearly nine months, when it finally became clear to me that I was in real danger of losing my mind, we were in church around New Year's Day. It was a special meeting of some kind, and the pastor brought out a big metal bowl and set it in the middle of the room, on the floor. He said, 'Some of us are carrying around burdens we ought to lay down. I'd like each of us to write down what we'll let go of in the coming year.'

"I looked at Carter, and I knew what he was thinking. I'd started to be a little more lucid about the whole thing lately, and I'd realized that I was holding onto that guilt like a baby's blanket. It was all I had left of him, I guess. But I also knew it was killing me and would destroy our mar- riage—destroy everything.

"I wrote, 'I will let go of my guilt. I will accept what has happened. Please, God, help me let go.'

"We dropped the slips of paper into the bowl, and the pastor struck a match to them. As I watched them burn, I felt a relief that I had not felt in all those months. Oh, it wasn't total or immediate, and I had plenty of hard times later—still do, actually, now and then—but I knew I had made a start.

"Please, Roger, make a start and come back to us, while you still can."

Pain comes with living. It's a fact that must be accepted. Unfortunately, some people seem to have more of it than others. But if pain can come, pain can go. In many cases the mere passing of time applies a great deal of balm. Other pains are more stubborn. Still, they must be dealt with.

In Moses 7:44, when Enoch is shown in vision that the whole world, except for Noah and his family, is to be de- stroyed in the Flood, he "wept over his brethren, and said unto the heavens: I will refuse to be comforted." Some people who have faced tragedy, especially when they feel responsible for someone else's suffering, are like Enoch —they "refuse to be comforted."

But the verse continues, ". . . the Lord said unto Enoch: Lift up your heart, and be glad; and look." In the ensuing verse, Enoch sees the yet-future coming of Christ to the earth to make his atonement and thereby replace pain and tragedy with joy and salvation.

People are tough and can overcome a lot of problems with willpower and determination. But there is some suffering that can be taken away in no other way than by turning it over to the one who suffered for all of us. He can heal not only the present and the future, but even the past.

2

I Didn't Know Life Would Be This Way: Handling the Present

Sometimes life is fulfilling and exciting. Sometimes it has more than its share of troubles and fears.

It must be a rare adult who doesn't occasionally host a parade of dark thoughts on a sleepless night. Maybe the cortege consists of thoughts of advancing age or death. Sometimes it's sorrow over lost dreams or opportunities. It could be about concerns or adjustments in relationships, such as children leaving home to go out on their own. Or perhaps it's just generalized worry or consternation that things didn't work out quite the way we thought they would in life.

Crises and worries and sorrows do come, even in the daylight. Of course, we hope that these are more than balanced out by joys and pleasant surprises and happiness and beauty. But balanced out or not, troubles will find us.

In these sober moments, life leads us toward one of two possible conclusions: Either we lean more and more toward the view that we are all merely pawns with little to say about what happens to us, or we find increasing evidence that there are things we can control, that we can make a difference, that constructive self-management is better than acquiescence to life's vicissitudes.

Either view is devoid of empirical proof, but I prefer the viewpoint that we are autonomous beings. Such a preference doesn't alleviate all possible pain—sometimes the burden of choice and control and self-management may, in fact, increase it—but autonomy and responsibility give purpose to our difficulties and poignancy to our joys.

The past is gone, the future is yet to arrive, and the present is the only time we really have. In the vignettes in this chapter, people struggle to make the most of it.

Primary and Secondary Control

Some days a missionary just knew he'd get mail. At least, on a few specific days during his month and five days in the Missionary Training Center, Elder Leonard had been right in his intuition. And today it was no surprise when the district leader came back to the classroom after a trip to the mailbox and handed him an envelope. Nor was it a surprise that the address was written in his dad's hand. Elder Leonard had clearly expected to hear from his dad today.

As he tore open the envelope, he thought back on the events of the last few days. It had only been three days since he'd learned of his changed assignment and he was trying his best to adjust, but adjustment wasn't easy. Being with a new district that had been here less than a week was tough, since he'd been here so much longer than they had. Feeling like a failure at French and having to be switched to English was hard, too. Hardest of all was facing the fact that he would not be going to France, the only place on earth he had ever wanted to go on a mission—where his father, mother, and grandfather had all served. To replace France with a stateside mission, still unassigned, was tough, after nineteen years of planning.

He took the letter from the envelope and started to read. "Dear Mel," it began. "By the time you read this, you'll probably be well settled into your new assignment."

Nope. Wrong there, Dad. Elder Leonard read on.

"When you called the other night, you were understandably disappointed, and your mom and I joined in your disappointment. We know how much you wanted to go to France, and you know how excited we were for you to be going where we had gone. But that is history now! I hope you know that a *changed* mission is not a *failed* mission.

"While we don't know why this change has occurred, we're confident that the Lord has other great things in store for you. Now—it's 'bucking up' time!

"I don't want to preach to you, but I'm sure you're already aware that how things turn out in this matter—and in most other matters—depends more on your own attitude than on anything else. The *events* are out of your control. How you look at them isn't. As with many things in life, we may not have primary control, that is, actual control over how things go, but we *always* have secondary control—how we look at things.

"It reminds me of the time when you were ten or twelve years old and we headed off for a summer vacation in Yellowstone Park, but the station wagon broke down in the Tetons, a few miles south of Yellowstone. Remember? We eventually had to be towed back to Jackson Hole to get the car fixed, and we never did make it to Yellowstone. You kids were really disappointed. We'd told you so much about the geysers and the bears you'd see.

"We spent an afternoon feeling sorry for ourselves, but the next morning, when we finally lifted our eyes and looked around at the gorgeous mountains and lakes and scenery, we decided we were in a great spot right there in the Tetons. But enjoying ourselves there wasn't automatic. It took a decision to do it. We had to decide to make the most of where we were.

"If that hadn't happened, we could have had a miserable stay in one of the most absolutely beautiful places on earth. This is how you're going to have to look at your mission change.

"I learned this lesson again in my work at the bank. Up until a few years ago I spent a lot of time waiting to be chosen for a higher position, like regional vice-president. Then one day I looked at my situation and decided I was coming to dislike the work I was doing because I was looking too hard at what I thought I wanted up ahead. And I realized that some things were really out of my control. All I could do was do my best at my present task and quit worrying about things I couldn't do anything about. I decided to 'enjoy the Tetons,' so to speak, and it made a big difference in my attitude.

"Well, I'll close with an old story that might help. Two people bought train tickets to St. Louis, but got on the wrong train. When they ended up in Kansas City one of them said, 'Well, this isn't where I was headed, but it doesn't look like a bad place. I think I'll like it.' The other one looked around and said, 'This isn't St. Louis, and I don't like it.' The attitude, not the location, made the difference."

Elder Leonard put down the letter with a smile. He wished he knew where his new assignment would be, but he was sure of one thing: it would probably be a lot more like Kansas City than Paris. Somehow, though, he was starting to feel that things were going to work out just fine.

"Enjoy the Tetons." Awfully good advice when we find ourselves with few options. The best way to handle the present is to try to control only what we actually can control.

It's true that we can't always exercise primary control. Sometimes matters are out of our hands. At those times our happiness depends on adjusting our thinking so that we can come to accept and like the place where we find ourselves. Some good advice comes from a group called Emotions Anonymous, which has as its motto, "Just for today, I will adjust myself to what *is*."

In contrast to this "bloom where you're planted" approach to life there is the contrary viewpoint that calls for going after what you want—also good advice in many situations. Deciding which of the two approaches to use at a given time can give us fits!

Indeed, some of life's most difficult decisions come in sorting out when to *try* for more and when to *settle* for what we have. Neither approach fits all of life's situations, and each has a cost. But when events are truly beyond our primary control, it's time to let the secondary control kick in, sit back, and enjoy the Tetons.

Taking Time to Gather Strength

Sister Nickel was well into her Relief Society lesson on service and compassion when a comment from JoAnne Lucken radically changed the direction of the discussion.

"Doesn't anybody besides me ever get *tired,* just plain tired of it all? I mean, I know it sounds whiny and selfish, but we're friends here, and I'm only saying that sometimes I feel like I'm all nurtured out!"

Sister Nickel laughed, along with the others. "Well, JoAnne, thanks for keeping us down to earth. I think we all know where you're coming from. And I think we ought to talk about that idea. What do you think, sisters? Sometimes we talk like all we have to do is go out and do all the good things we see need to be done, and everything will be fine. Well, is it that simple? What happens when we just plain wear out?"

JoAnne spoke again. "I heard someone call it 'compassion fatigue.' I think it's a good term for what I'm talking about—wearing out, even when you're doing good things."

"There's also 'kid fatigue,' " one woman added.

"And 'husband fatigue,' " another laughed.

"What about just plain 'fatigue'?" another sister asked.

Sister Nickel said, "I think we all feel fatigue of some kind at times. Maybe what we ought to be asking is, what do we do about it? How do we gather strength, if you will?"

After a moment one woman said, "Well, even Jesus went into the desert for forty days at one point. I think part of the reason was to gather strength. But I don't suppose most of us are in a position to take six weeks off! Still, maybe the principle applies to us, too."

"I think it does," Sister Nickel said. "Solitude, a retreat from things, a time to plan and think and ponder—these things are necessary, as hard as they are to come by."

"They *are* hard to come by," JoAnne said. "With four kids, a busy husband, a job, Church callings—you know, the same things most of you face—it's hard to find the time for anything close to planning, let alone solitude!"

"But you have to *make* the time for it," a woman said. "In the mission field it's called Preparation Day, P-day. We all need a P-day. I take mine on Saturday mornings. I get up early and spend time reading scriptures and planning and thinking. A friend of mine stays up late one night a week to do the same thing. It's better than nothing."

"Good idea, Louise," Sister Nickel said. "We need some kind of mental retreat."

Louise went on. "When I was on my mission I had to learn not to feel the full responsibility for the 135,000 people in my area. I mean, I had to do my best and do all I could do to bring them the gospel. But doing my best is different from taking on myself the responsibility of their using their free agency in a way different from what I hoped for them. Now I have to fight that same kind of guilt when I'm overburdened and have to say no to a new request—even from the Church."

"Mothers aren't supposed to say no," JoAnne said.

"But you have to," Louise said. "Sometimes you just have to."

We can become weary of things, of routine, of change, of social expectations, of relationships, and yes, even of compassion. The world has a way of wearing us out, even when we're doing good. And if we're not careful, our well can run dry.

Even when we put others first, we must remember to fill our own cup—for only then can we pour into others'. Our stewardship for self isn't selfish. It must include service to others, but when a person feels drained, the shell of self is hollowed out and nobody is served. Saying a few "nos" now can help us say a lot more "yeses" later. Only by remaining whole can we offer to others not only what we have but also what we are.

Reading, pondering, praying, planning, even saying no when we must—all are aspects of the rejuvenation and strength-gathering process all of us need on a regular basis. And it's never too late to start renewing.

Physical Limits and Mental Effects

When the doorbell rang Vivian called, "Come in!" and stayed where she was on the couch.

"Vivian, it's Marla." Her neighbor came down the hallway and into the living room, where Vivian sat. "How are you doing, hon?"

"Oh, I'm not too bad today. I made it through the morning pretty good. With any luck I'll get a nap before Arlin gets back with the kids."

"Oh, where are they?"

"Here, sit down, Marla." Vivian motioned her to a chair. "He took them with him to visit while he helps Grandpa roto-till his garden this afternoon. What have you got there?"

Marla sat across from Vivian, holding a newspaper clipping. "Vivian, I know you've told me a lot about your disease, or your problem, whatever it is, but I guess I didn't really understand a lot about it until I saw this in the *Journal* this morning." She handed Vivian the clipping. "Is this what you have?"

Vivian looked at the paper. The headline read, "CFIDS —The Sick and Tired Disease."

"That's it, all right—CFIDS: chronic fatigue and immune dysfunction syndrome." She read the article silently, nodding her head several times along the way. "That's me, one hundred percent," she said at the end. "My doctors usually call mine CFS—chronic fatigue syndrome, but it's the same. There's also chronic Epstein-Barr virus—CEBV. There's ME—myalgic encephalomyelitis. They're all the same, or at least the symptoms are—you're deadly tired *all* the time, like I am. You know me—I get tired sitting still! And cold. Look at me, wrapped in a sweater, when everybody else is talking about how hot it's been this spring."

Marla nodded. She'd seen Vivian's problem up close for the three years they'd been neighbors. Some days Vivian really couldn't function, and even on her good days she moved at half-speed. "Well," Marla said, "it's not something a lot of people know much about. I know I'd never heard of it until I met you!"

"And you probably thought I was pretty weird at first, didn't you?"

"Well . . . ," Marla started. "I didn't know anything about what you had, and . . ."

"Everybody thought I was wacko, Marla. I know that, and I don't blame them—I did, too!" Vivian said. "Really! I mean, what do you think when you suddenly turn from a normal twenty-two-year-old young mother into a lethargic, irritable, aching person who can barely get out of bed in the morning, and who is always freezing to boot!

"I mean, Arlin thought I was having some kind of a mental breakdown. I know he did, even though he never said it.

"I was depressed a lot. It's depressing, you know! They give you all these tests and tell you it isn't this and it isn't that, and pretty soon you start to think it's only in your head, and even that it's somehow your own *fault* you're this way. And to hear my own sister call me an attention-seeking hypochondriac . . ." Vivian choked up a little, then went on.

"For a long time I thought I could make it go away by trying harder, that I could become normal if I had enough willpower. But it didn't work. I was sick!

"It was so hard not to know what it was. And now, in the last few years, to at least get a name, or several names, for it—well, that helps a lot. At least now I can say to people that I have something—a real disease. It's a lot better than having to say, 'I'm just tired all the time.' "

Having a label to put on her problems helped Vivian enormously. And it helped others, too, to finally accept that she had a "real" problem.

Vivian's rare and frustrating ailment dramatically illustrated how inseparably connected are our physical selves and our emotional, spiritual, and mental selves. The connection between mind and body has been illustrated in research that shows a drop in death rates of up to thirty-five percent in the elderly right before birthdays and holidays —and a corresponding increase immediately after these events. Anticipation alone can keep people alive.

But positive thinking has its limits and its dangers. One danger is that we will not accept what needs accepting and will push ourselves in an attempt to overcome actual ailments—mental or physical—by "trying harder." Our failure to achieve the impossible then makes us more anxious and depressed, worsening and continuing the cycle.

Knowing when to accept and live within required limitations is evidence of wisdom. Those who handle life well are those who learn how to adjust their thinking about how things are, even when the prospects are not what we would choose them to be.

Few Things Are Ever Settled Once and for All

Everywhere I turn I find the same pattern, Todd thought. Sort of like hearing a new word—you'd swear it was new, anyway—then in the next few days you hear and read it everywhere! It had to have been there all along, of course, but it somehow went unnoticed.

Well, this week's theme was how things never got settled or finished, and how much that bothered him lately.

Todd was watching a football game on TV, but his mind was a million miles from the techniques of the quarterback. He guessed it had started with two conversations he'd overheard simultaneously on the commuter train yesterday morning. The first was about investments and the need, according to the two people talking, to constantly reevaluate where your money was resting.

"That's the problem," the young woman in a business suit had said. "Working money can't rest. It needs to be active, to keep turning over."

"Well," her male companion had said, "there are stable investments, of course."

"Oh, sure," the woman responded, "low-risk, low-yield things. But I'm talking about high-powered stuff—where you get in fast and get out fast. Money needs to *move*."

At the same time, on the other side of the car, two older women were talking about family matters. One of them said, "I guess I was naive. I thought when Jessica—my last one—left home my child-rearing days were over, even though I'd heard people say that you worry as much or more about your grown kids as you did when they were little."

"It's true," the other woman said.

"And now Jessica's back home with her two-year-old, so I'm still raising kids."

Somehow, these conversations tied in with what Todd had been thinking—or probably feeling, more than thinking—lately. Maybe it was middle-agedness or something, but he'd found himself frustrated that nothing seemed permanent. He had painted all morning on the outside of the house—all the while reflecting that he had done the same job just a few years ago. And he'd noticed rust spots on the car he'd paid a small fortune for not so long ago. He was also worried that he was getting out of touch with his profession. He'd thought he'd kept up, through annual conventions and occasional classes, yet now and then he'd hear younger managers talking about concepts he was aware of but didn't feel very familiar with. He knew what the terms meant, but they weren't second-nature with him as they were with them.

Even in church there were sometimes new emphases and attitudes—subtle as the changes often were—that made him have to question his life-long views.

All of this bothered him. Somehow, he wanted to have things stop and stand still for a while so he could catch his breath. But it wasn't until right now that he'd hooked all these feelings and observations together. Now he'd put his finger on it: His real concern was that nothing ever really got settled.

To the young, life sometimes seems like a series of events to get past. "When I finish elementary school . . . junior high . . . high school . . ." "After my mission . . . college . . ." "After the kids are raised . . . the house is paid for . . ."

After this, after that. But Todd is discovering that after this comes more of this. After that, more of that. Life *isn't* a series of events to get past. Much of life is repetition, even boring repetition. Most things are never settled once and for all.

Much of what we call fact changes, too. The amazing events in eastern Europe in the fall of 1989, for instance, including the dismantling of the Berlin Wall, free elections in numerous communist countries, the overthrow of long-entrenched ideologies and rulers—how quickly these all occurred! It's as if westerners woke up one morning to find their traditional enemies looking more like allies. Millions of people opted for greater freedom, and got it—with all its promise and all its trials.

Even science has to change its views. How many times have we been told that there could never be two identical snowflakes? Yet, in 1988 scientists reported the accidental discovery of two snowflakes that were alike in every way.

I once heard a doctor comment that in medicine *mastery* isn't spoken of, rather *practice* is used—because the profession is always growing and advancing. Life can be frustrating for those who desire to do a thing once or think a thought once or take a stand once—and be done with it. In this life things are seldom settled. That, we must settle for.

Handling Stress

"But Dr. Cox," Julie exclaimed, "you tell me to reduce the stress in my life, and all that does is *increase* it! How do I reduce stress when I have two active teenagers and three younger kids, a husband who has to be out of town most of every week, a part-time job, Church callings . . ."

"Whoa, whoa," Dr. Cox laughed. "You're getting *me* stressed out just listening to you!"

Julie laughed, too.

"Let's sit down and talk about this a minute," Dr. Cox said. "Come into the office." Dr. Cox led the way from the examination room, and they sat down across the desk from each other.

Julie spoke first. "Look, Doctor, I know what you're saying, but I don't see how I can do much about it at this point in my life."

"If you don't do something about it, Julie," Dr. Cox said, "it might affect the quality of the rest of your life. From what you just said, it seems to me you think stress comes from outside events."

"Well, doesn't it?" Julie asked. "I mean, send me to a warm beach for a couple of weeks and then see if you can even *find* my blood pressure on the bottom of the scale."

"That's not necessarily how it works, though. A study shows that people with type A personalities—you know, the hard-driving, ambitious, competitive types—are more likely to rate their jobs as stressful even if they do the same job as type Bs—the more easy-going types. This indicates that it isn't the outside event as much as a person's *view* of the events. The type As can sit on that same beach with you and be stressed about what they're supposed to be doing back home!"

"I can relate to that," Julie said.

"Even exercise—thought to be an element in stress reduction—doesn't help some people; only changing their view of the world helps."

"Changing their view of the world?"

"Yes, getting them to think about their situation and take a different view of reality," Dr. Cox said. "Here's my prescription for stress reduction, Julie." Dr. Cox wrote for a moment on a sheet of paper and then handed it to her. On it was written:

1. Exercise—regularly
2. Meditate—imagine peaceful scenes
3. Laugh—regularly
4. Relax—deeply and regularly
5. Change your thinking

"I understand all of these except for the last one," Julie said. "What is it I'm supposed to change in my thinking?"

"First, get it out of your head that the world is doing this to you. Life is stressful, true. And it takes a certain amount of stress just to be able to function properly. But people blow things way out of proportion.

"I suppose a physician has as much possibility of negative stress as anybody. The way I handle it is to ask myself two questions. I call them perspective questions.

"First, 'Just how much does this situation or event really matter anyway?' Second, 'How can I make the most of—even benefit from—the situation?' It's surprising how few things really matter enough to get upset over. And by way of looking for benefit, it's interesting how much less frustrating it is to wait in traffic when I use the time to play an educational tape in my car, for example, or to listen to good music. Just by asking myself these two questions, I can let a lot of things go and feel much more in control."

Julie's first reaction to her doctor's advice to reduce stress is typical. Most people associate stress with outside events, many of which they can't do much about. But while surroundings certainly do play a role, Dr. Cox is correct when he says that the viewpoint of the individual is the critical thing.

Points to consider about stress are the following:

First, *stressors*—causes of stress—are, in themselves, neutral. If we react positively to them, they keep us going. Stress is defined as merely a state of bodily or mental tension, a certain amount of which is necessary in order to cause us to get out of bed each morning and face the day. "Good stress" or "moderate stress" causes us to meet, and want to meet, the challenges of life. It motivates and drives us to do a good job.

Second, stressors only result in "bad stress" when they exist in quantities that we perceive as unmanageable. Then we feel out of control, and our driving force to do well becomes the fear of failure. Eventually, the body reacts the way Julie's did, with stomach upsets and other problems. What would be motivating under "good stress" becomes, under "bad stress," debilitating, or at least weakening.

For example, the "good stress" which causes an employee to perform well on most days may turn to "bad stress" when the supervisor stops by to observe the work. A cook who has prepared an acceptable, routine meal may suddenly feel a great increase in tension when told that esteemed guests will be coming by.

Third, an estimated twenty to twenty-five percent of the population handles stress sufficiently poorly as to suffer from depression or anxiety at a significant level. These people have lost control. Life for them is no longer merely a challenge, but a difficult, nearly overwhelming struggle. They have lost the ability to adapt. The major signs of depression are: loss of interest in life, disturbed eating and sleeping habits, energy loss—or frenetic energy increase, and feelings of helplessness or hopelessness. People displaying a number of these characteristics need professional help.

Fourth, not only negative events but also those we call good are stressors. For instance, too many clients requesting services can cause stress in a professional or a craftsman as easily as too few. Inheriting sudden wealth or winning the lottery can be an extreme stressor.

One study shows that, for those with low self-esteem, image-enhancing events—like a promotion or a marriage engagement—also cause a great deal of stress. These events create incongruities in such a person's own view of himself. A person who feels like a loser just can't win!

Fifth, a whole bunch of small, daily hassles can have the same cumulative effect as a few large stressors.

Probably most of us have seen the Holmes stress scale, which assigns points to stressors—100 for the death of a spouse, 73 for a divorce, and so on. But let's say that driving in heavy traffic irritates you and you have to face it twice a day. Maybe it would only be equivalent to a two or a three on the scale, but these points add up. Add to that a troublesome colleague at the office who bugs you at least five times a day—ten points. Then there's a particular kind of report you fervently hate to make out, yet it has to be done weekly—a fifteen.

Get the idea? You are being pecked to death by pigeons —which may be just as wracking as being devoured whole by a sea serpent!

Sixth, some things in our environment *can* be changed. Better organization and better communication with others may improve stressful situations a great deal. Commuting in your own car might be avoided by joining a car pool or riding public transportation. But remember that more important than what happens is how we view what happens. And realism says we won't be able to remove all tensions through working things out. Some things simply have to be tolerated. Acceptance alone can reduce stressful feelings.

Finally, no scale can fit each of us. What is merely irritating for one is a catastrophe for another. And the quiet, outwardly secure type isn't necessarily better off—and is sometimes worse off—than the person who weeps and wails and lets it all out.

Besides Dr. Cox's two perspective questions, there's a third one that often helps. After "How much does it really matter?" and "How can I benefit from it?" ask yourself, "What's the worst outcome that can possibly result from this event?"

Sometimes it's amazing how easy it is to settle right down and reduce your own stress by stopping to think. It helps to realize that being five minutes late to a movie, as much as you hate to miss the credits, or having to scrape (or scrap) a piece of toast, as irritating as it is that the toaster adjustment is suddenly acting strange, is not going to alter the course of history very much.

3

Moving On: Preparing for the Future

Our expectations and beliefs—how we look at things—
make so much difference in how things turn out in life. It's
like looking at the Grand Canyon through a camera: the
canyon is there, it's the reality. But how we see it depends
on the type of lens and filters on the camera at the time. It's
the same way for each person as he views the world—
there is no such thing as an objective view. We see through
the lenses of our own biases, views, fears, desires, and past
experiences, and these make all the difference in how and
what we see.

A person who "sees" that he can prepare for, and be in
charge of, his own future is bound to "find" a different kind
of future than the one who carries around a set of negative
beliefs about himself.

Bob Kall says, "Guido the plumber and Michelangelo obtained their marble from the same quarry, but what each saw in the marble made the difference between a nobleman's sink and a brilliant sculpture." Guido and Michelangelo "saw" things differently. What the marble became didn't depend on the marble, but on the vision in the eyes of the craftsman.

The world has need of good sinks, of course, but how many lives have been turned into something less than they might have been because of a lack of vision? And on the other hand, how many lives have been enriched by the belief in self, even if that belief originally came from an outside source? An employee at General Motors once said, "My foreman thinks I have more ability than I think I have. So I consistently do better work than I thought I could do."

The future is ours. But only if we believe in ourselves and prepare for it. Think of it this way: What has been, has been—but what will be, need not be.

Decisiveness is vital in determining our futures. We will never have all the facts. At some point we have to make the leap of faith and say, "This is what I *want* to do, and this is what I *will* do."

As you make your own preparations to "move on," the vignettes below may help.

Moving On—The Time Comes

"That's enough for now," Lura thought, as she finished dusting the empty china hutch in the dining room. "I'd better get lunch on the table."

"Lura!" Henry's voice came up the stairs, as it had several times this morning.

"Yes, Henry?" Lura called back.

"Lura!" Henry called more loudly.

"Henry, I hear you," Lura answered more loudly.

"Lura!"

Lura stepped to the top of the stairs and called back, "What is it, Henry?"

By now her husband was at the foot of the stairs and there was no more need for shouting. "Lura, I called you three times. You must be going deaf," he said.

When Lura could only laugh, Henry looked puzzled for a moment. Then he grinned, recognizing that they had re-lived the old joke—again. There was no need for her to re-peat the punch line—"And I answered you all three times, dear." The joke was even better considering it was Henry, not Lura, who had started losing his hearing twenty years before, and they both knew it.

"I need you to look at this junk in the boys' room," Henry said. They still called it "the boys' room," even though their last boy had left home many years before. They had also avoided it until now and had cleaned out the rest of the house first.

"Do you want lunch first?"

"Sounds good," Henry said as he started up the stairs.

"Feels good to sit down," Henry said during lunch. "We're about through up here, aren't we?"

"Everything's boxed," Lura said. "I'm glad we started early." Her voice echoed slightly in the nearly empty din-ing area. The woman looked around her. "The place is as bare as the day we moved in," she said.

It wasn't easy, especially for Lura, to move from the home they had lived in for thirty-eight years, the home where they had raised their family. But it was time, and they had found a condominium only three blocks away. This made the task easier, and they had decided to pack and haul their goods one load at a time, in their own car, doing as much as they felt like in a given day. It felt better that way, and it gave them a chance to go through things carefully, so as not to take anything they really wouldn't need. In a few days a crew would come with a truck and move the furniture, and they would be finished.

The idea of a smaller place, with no stairs to climb, no lawn to mow, and no snow to shovel, had its appeal, but it did not come without mixed feelings. Roots can go awfully deep after thirty-eight years. They especially had for Lura, who had moved often as a child, and had always wanted to "settle down." Yet Lura had been the one to make the decision that it was time to go.

One day in the early summer, three or four months back, after seeing her husband come back into the house from some heavy spring garden and yard clean-up work that was almost too much for him, she said, "Sit down, Henry." They sat in the darkened living room, in which the shades were kept drawn during the summer to keep out the heat, and she said, "Henry, we've got to go."

"Huh? Go where?"

"Just go. Move. Find another place." Henry said nothing, and she couldn't see his face clearly. She went on. "It's either that or they're going to carry one of us out of here one of these days. And the other one will *have* to go, then."

That was it, direct and to the point, as was Lura's style. There wasn't a lot more to say. They both knew she was right. A moment later she went back to her kitchen chores and no more was said. But late that night, Henry awoke to the sound of crying. When he put his arms around Lura, she said, "It's hard to think of moving for the last time in our lives." Henry had tried not to think about it until she said that. But then he lay awake long after his wife's sobs had turned to steady, even breathing.

Only one time since then had there been any outward emotion shown, and that was when, during the packing and sorting of the collected treasures of two lifetimes, they had come to the Christmas ornaments and myriad other miscellaneous things stored under the stairs. Much of it would be offered to the children, making the discarding less final. But when Lura had filled two boxes with scraps and reminders of the past that would be of no value to anyone else, she broke down. She had allowed herself a minute's tears, before calling Henry to "take this junk away."

His use of the term "junk" in the boys' room today had, therefore, special meaning. They both knew how hard cleaning out that room would be, but they had delayed long enough.

"Ready to go look at that junk?" she asked as she pushed herself back from the table.

We can let the future overtake us, or we can go out and meet it. It's like the difference in keeping a surfboard on the crest of the wave or letting the wave overtake it.

"Moving on" can be tough at any age. And certain moves are worse than others, because they so clearly close a chapter of life. Yet, when the move is inevitable, how wise it is to take control as Lura has done. As hard as parting with their memory-laden keepsakes must be, she and Henry will survive and even thrive on the move because they took it into their own hands, which put them in charge of their own happiness.

Taking control of our own future doesn't always happen without pain. Still, it's the best option we have.

Roots go deep, but when a living thing has to be moved, there's a difference between uprooting with a yank and gently working the roots loose, leaving them able to grow again in new soil. As much as possible, people ought to do their own transplanting.

To Whom Are You Still Proving Yourself, and Why?

"Ted, I don't know how we got into this conversation, but I'm not trying to start anything."

"What is it you're saying, Rae?" Ted tried to keep the anger out of his voice, but he knew he wasn't successful.

"I'm saying you're different when your mother's here. Maybe I'm the same way around my folks, I don't know. But when your mom's here, I feel kind of left out. I guess that's part of what I'm trying to say."

"Are you *jealous* of my mother, for heaven's sake?"

"Don't let her hear you, Ted. No, I don't think I'm jealous at all. It's that you kind of act like, well, like we're—the kids and I—not wanted or not important or something, when you're around your relatives."

"Rae, you're my wife. Why would you think . . . ? I mean, I happen to have a mother, too, you know."

"I know," Rae said.

"I don't see her very often, and maybe I give her more attention when she's here for a few days, but that doesn't mean anything about you or the kids."

"I know."

Ted was calmer now. After a pause he said, "But you think I'm different when she's here?"

"Yes, you are. I don't even know how, but maybe it's sort of like you're younger or something."

"Younger? So you're saying I'm immature?"

"No," Rae laughed. "I do think she treats you like you're still a kid sometimes, though."

"Once a mother, always a mother, I guess," Ted said.

"You want to know what I really think it is?" Rae asked.

"Okay," Ted replied quickly.

"I think you're still proving yourself to her."

"What? How?"

"Remember the potato-mashing contest?"

"What?" Ted asked. "What are you talking about?"

"It happened the last time she was here, last year," Rae said. "You were helping—both of you were helping—with Sunday dinner. I asked you to mash the potatoes. You started getting out the electric mixer. She was standing right there at the counter, and she started pulling out drawers. Suddenly she pulled out the masher—you know, the old heavy wire masher with the wooden handle. I use it all the time when I mash potatoes, but you never do."

"I don't remember any of this," Ted said.

"Well, your mom said, 'Don't you use this?' 'No,' you said. 'It's better,' she said, 'and faster.' " Rae paused.

"And?" Ted asked.

"You said, 'Hey, I'm doing this. Let me do it my way.' Your mom turned away and busied herself with setting the table."

"Well," Ted said, "I do remember now that she said something that bothered me."

"Honey, I'm not your psychoanalyst, you know, but that's what I mean about 'proving yourself.' I've suggested before that you use the masher, too, but you've never answered *me* that way. You might have said you didn't want to use it, but not in that tone or with the phrase, 'Let me do it my way.' "

"Probably not," Ted said.

"I know I do it, too," Rae said. "I nearly bit my dad's head off a few years ago when he said some innocuous thing about money. I took it as snooping into our affairs. I think I was 'proving myself,' somehow."

We've probably all been in "potato-mashing contests" with our parents at one time or another. If "once a mother, always a mother," is true, so is "once a child, always a child." How deep the ruts run! How easy they are to fall back into when we're reintroduced to the parent/child setting!

In our youth we may spend a lot of effort trying to make our parents or other adults proud of us, and perhaps an equal amount trying to prove ourselves to them—or to prove that we are free of them. When we need their help, they're indispensable; when we don't, they're in the way. Yet their subconscious presence is never removed from our lives.

It may take nearly a lifetime for both generations to feel like full equals with each other. But it's a worthy goal, and in taking charge of our own future we must eventually come to the point where we're no longer in need of "Let me do it my way" statements.

Is Time Getting Away from Me?

It was 9:04 Saturday morning, a beautiful spring day, and Jane was frustrated already. She stood at the kitchen table—no time to sit down—bending over her "Perfect Planner," pencil in hand, scratching out and rearranging. She was already two hours and four minutes behind her perfect schedule for that day, not counting the many plans she had failed to accomplish during the past week.

"This thing is going to drive me nuts," she thought. "I feel less organized now than before I got a planner, and I'm not sure I get any more done now. I know I'm more frustrated about what I *don't* get done."

Jane had set a New Year's resolution to be more organized. When she saw the "Perfect Planner" in a bookstore, she was sure she'd found the answer. She bought the planner and hurried home to fill it up. She listed goals and plans for the year, the month, the week, and the day—

each level becoming progressively more detailed and programmed. Each hour was filled and accounted for.

That was a great day! She hadn't felt so much in control of her life for years. She even remembered the date—January 18. She slept well that night, knowing that the next day would start a new era in her life—she was going to get so much more done this year than last!

The first problem occurred before sunrise the next morning when her eighth-grade son missed the school bus. At eight o'clock, when her planner said she should be starting aerobic exercises, she was just pulling away from the school. The thought crossed her mind to stop at the bread store while she was in the neighborhood, but she'd scheduled her shopping for the *next* day, so she hurried home to get back on schedule. The day went pretty well after that, except she noticed that normal family interruptions bothered her more than usual, and by evening she felt a bit guilty about the things she hadn't accomplished.

She realized she'd been too tight with her scheduling and that she'd have to leave leeway for family and others who needed to be able to make demands on her time.

In the next month, Jane found satisfaction in crossing off tasks and goals she'd finished. But she also had a nagging feeling of never doing as much as she should. Her response was to plan more carefully and to squeeze every minute dry, staying up later and getting up earlier.

Her family started to tease her about whether they could be fitted into her schedule now and then. Her suggestion that they might *all* benefit from a planner was met with everything from silence (husband) to hoots (eighth-grader) to scorn (twelfth-grader).

Jane worried even more about her attempts to control her time when her mother called her one day and asked, with a certain tone, if she happened to have time to talk—a question she'd never asked before. Jane had to wonder what image she was projecting.

As she stood looking at her planner that morning, she thought back on the previous week. She had turned down a luncheon invitation with an old friend because she was "behind" on her schedule. She had stayed up Wednesday night until 12:30, working on goals, and she still hadn't managed to catch up. She'd been tired ever since and not very *interested* in catching up, which made her feel guilty.

And, the previous night her twelfth-grade son had shown her a lost-and-found ad in the paper from a person who said he'd lost his planner. "Reward offered. I can't function without it!" the ad said. Her son had added wryly, "Just like you, Mom."

Suddenly her planner didn't seem so "perfect" anymore. Maybe she'd become a slave to it. Maybe her need to plan didn't come from a desire to accomplish more or to enjoy life more, but from some personality compulsion. She didn't like the thought.

On an impulse—something her planner frowned on—Jane called her family to the kitchen and had them each place a hand on a corner of her planner. "What are we doing, Mom? Taking a oath to be more perfect planners?" her eighth-grader asked sarcastically. How amazed and delighted they all were when she answered, "Ready, set, *rip!*" She didn't have to say it twice. In seconds, the book was in a hundred pieces, thrown around the kitchen. Strangely, this event brought the most satisfying feeling Jane had had since "Day One," January 18. She would sleep well that night.

At the same instant, across the street, Paula sat on the couch, frustrated. Her life was out of control. The past week she'd felt like a victim. Thinking about it made her tired.

First, on Monday, she'd heard of a mall sale. She had wasted half a day at it, and she had come away dissatisfied with the ratio of dollars saved to time spent.

And twice this week she'd demonstrated once again that she didn't know how to say no. The first time was when she agreed to be on yet another PTA committee. The second time was when her husband insisted that she watch a three-night TV miniseries with him. The presentation was adequate, but she never really got into it. It seemed like a two-hour movie stretched to six—matched by an equal amount of advertising.

She felt so unorganized and out of control. Whatever came along, she did, without any thought or planning. Procrastination was a specialty of hers. Her mental list of things she wanted and needed to do seemed endless, and guilt-producing.

Suddenly the thought came to Paula, What I need is a planner like Jane was talking about the other day! The "Perfect Planner," I think she called the one she likes so well. Then I won't be a slave to the demands of things and others anymore.

I'll get one next week, she thought, then corrected herself. That's your problem, girl—procrastination. I'll do it right now.

She grabbed the car keys, called to her husband that she'd be right back, and got into the car. As she backed out of the driveway, she waved at her neighbor Jane, who was at the garbage can. Jane was emptying a small trash basket that looked half full of scraps of paper. She was smiling.

Both Jane and Paula feel frustrated and enslaved—Jane by excessive planning, and Paula by the lack of planning.

Each woman has overreacted. Notice that they both responded to feelings of guilt. Guilt is not the healthiest motivator and shouldn't be a big factor in causing us either to become frantic planners or to reject planning altogether. There really is a middle ground which would help both Jane and Paula be effective and goal-oriented, but which would still leave room for spontaneity and relaxation.

Here are some thoughts on time use and planning:

First, there *are* no *perfect planners*—no magic books or programs that can take care of all our time problems. How we use time depends not only on our planning skills and the procedures we follow but also on our own personalities, desires, and ways of looking at life. It also depends on our availability to others. If we too often put up the "Busy —Do Not Disturb" sign for our family and friends, they will get a message we may come to regret having sent.

Second, overplanning is as bad as underplanning. We can't do everything, and overload isn't healthy. Happy people are seldom frantic people. Some of them even know how to waste a perfectly good afternoon and feel no guilt whatsoever!

Third, any plan needs to be flexible. Let the little things take care of themselves. As surely as the lack of planning makes us slaves to the demands of others, there is also a tyranny to even the best plans when they take over our lives, requiring us to consult them before we dare sit back and watch the sunset.

Fourth, just because you have *time* to chair a library committee doesn't mean you have to say yes to that—or any other—request. Your time is yours, to spend as you will. Your time is your life. Give your life only to the things you truly believe in.

And finally, carefully-laid plans can help us get a lot done, but that alone isn't the purpose of planning. We must feel good about the things we're doing, and equally good about the things we're choosing to leave undone. Good time use plus wise choices equal future happiness.

Commitments Without Passion

"Whaddya think of this weather, Earl?" Arlie called over the backyard fence to his neighbor.

Earl looked up from where he was kneeling in a flower bed. "Say, if I was a pessimist, I'd say it'll snow tomorrow."

Arlie laughed. "It is a little too good, isn't it? Especially for so early in the year."

"But I'll take it while it's here," Earl said. "I've not seen a prettier start to spring in years. I guess you're getting your place in shape to sell, aren't you?"

"Oh, we're getting it in shape, all right," Arlie answered, "but not to sell. Changed our minds."

"What's that?" Earl stood up and came over closer to the fence. "You're not selling?"

"Nope, you'll have to put up with us maybe *another* thirty years."

"Why, last I heard . . ."

"I know, I know, Earl. We told everybody last fall we were going to build. But now we've thought better of it. Going to stay right here, if you'll let us."

"What changed your mind? Cost?"

"Oh, that partly, I suppose," Arlie said, "but mostly I think we never really wanted to build at all. It was something we talked about when we were younger. You know, Jen would say, 'Wouldn't it be nice—when we build—to have a deck out back?' Or I'd say, 'When we build we'll put in a sprinkler system with a timer.'

"It was just a phrase we used—'when we build.' I suspect that at one point, when we were young, we probably wanted to, so we could have things the way we wanted. It got to be a way of talking after that."

"Well, my, my. When or how did you come to this insight that saved you a small fortune and kept me from having to break in a new neighbor?" Earl asked.

"Well, Jen was talking to a friend who said something about what a lot of work it can be to keep an eye on a project like this. I'd always planned on being the contractor myself, and hiring the subcontractors. Well, the woman was telling Jen all the troubles they'd had in that situation, and Jen told me about it. I'd known it could be a hassle, but I still thought building was something we wanted to do.

"But in talking about it I asked Jen if she was sure she wanted to go through with it. She hesitated just long enough for me to figure out that we'd never really talked about actually going through with it. She told me later she hadn't wanted to do it for several years, but she thought *I* did. And I told her the same thing!

"Building was an idea we were in love with, but we'd never thought about the reality. It was easy to talk about it when we were young and couldn't afford to anyway, but now that we *could* do it, we'd never really talked it through. Neither of us wanted to be the one to squelch what we thought was the other one's dream."

Earl chuckled, and Arlie went on.

"And we got to wondering if we wanted to tie ourselves to a big project—and to another twenty years of mortgage payments—at this point in our lives. We decided the answer was no. Now all we have to do is figure out what we *do* want to do. Jen wants to take flying lessons, for starters."

"Well, what do you know!" Earl said. "And I thought I *knew* you people."

"Says she's always wanted to fly. Just never thought talking about it made a lot of sense before. Now, she says, why not?"

Arlie and Jen have made an important discovery— what they don't want to do. Now they're on their way to step two—finding what they do want to do.

Fortunately, this couple was saved from the pitfalls of the so-called Abilene paradox—the theory of group behavior that explains how a group can proceed toward an end that no individual in the group believes in. Its name comes from a fifty-three-mile trip a family made years ago to Abilene, Texas, on a 104-degree day, in a car with no air-conditioning or shock absorbers, in order to eat in the Good Luck Café. The trip was a disaster, and in the ensuing family fight it became clear that *no one* had wanted to go! Nobody spoke up because each one thought everybody else wanted to make the trip!

Families and individuals run the risk of having the Abilene paradox dictate their choices and their behaviors. To avoid that danger, it's important to frequently evaluate and reassess goals and commitments and to keep asking, "What do I really want to commit myself to? What really makes me happy? Why am I doing what I'm doing?"

Commitments are a bridge from the present to the future. Before we pay the toll and start across, we must be sure we really want to arrive at the other side.

Dream and Dare

The speaker stood before his audience. "They call me a 'motivational speaker,' and that must mean I'm supposed to help you want to do something. The thing is, I don't *know* what it is you want to do—only you can know that. But I might be able to help you take the first step. And the first one is by far the biggest one.

"I'm going to tell you today how I came to be standing here. As with all success stories, I'll have to go back and tell you about my pre-success days. They weren't exactly days of failure. I was never quite like the guys in those full-page magazine ads who say, 'Five years ago I was living in a two-hundred-dollar flat in Cleveland . . .'

"In fact, my story has nothing to do with money, and I'm not selling anything. But five years ago I wasn't doing what I wanted to do in life, and now I am. And that's success. My story has a lot to do with happiness and change and growth.

"Five years ago I had what people would call a 'good job'—secure, paying fairly well, benefits, good people to work with. But there was no real challenge, no potential, no excitement to it. I'd pretty well decided that that was how life was, and that I would just make the most of it and wait for retirement. But at forty I was a long way from the gold watch ceremony.

"One day I went to a funeral where the deceased was praised for having given up his own interests—trying for a profession in singing—years before, in exchange for what was called a 'more reasonable, mature approach': settling down to support his family. The speaker said the man had always missed the singing, but that he knew his duty.

"I didn't think much about it until later the same day when I bumped into an old friend, who was, in fact, in town for the funeral. We talked about our lives and interests, and he mentioned he had volunteered as a baseball umpire in a kids' league, and said how much he loved it. He was studying up so that he could take a test and try to move to a higher level.

"Well, he was an athlete at heart, and I knew he'd wanted to be a pro, when he was young. I thought it was great that he was staying with something he loved, even if on a lesser scale.

"I went home that night and started thinking. One man had been buried with praise for giving up what he'd really wanted to do. Another had managed to keep his hand in his interests.

"I got to wondering why the first man couldn't have

stayed in singing, even if only on an amateur level. Why did he have to give it up entirely?

"Then it hit me—what about me? At my funeral would they be saying I'd given up my dreams for duty? Or wouldn't my life be better off if I found a way to accomplish some of my dreams that were rapidly being pushed further and further back?

"It took me awhile even to dare to resurrect my dreams. What came to me was how much I'd always wanted to travel. And I'd done some when I was younger. But later, with a family, it was hard to afford the kind of travel I had in mind. How, I asked myself, could I find a way to do it?

"Well, to make this short, there are ways to get into travel, such as leading tours, without selling the farm and cashing in the pension. It doesn't have to be all or nothing. And it's worked out nicely for me. The travel led to the speaking, and here I am. I may not ever get to do all the traveling I wanted to earlier in my life, but I've done a lot more than I would have if I hadn't made the decision to get started.

"Decision—that's the key. A man once said to me, 'Boy, I wish I could go to Europe,' implying that he didn't have the money.

"I said, 'Your "Europe" is sitting in your driveway.' He grinned when he got my message. His camper and truck cost as much as three or four of my trips to Europe. Now don't get me wrong, I'm not saying my trips are of more value than his recreational vehicle. But it illustrates the choice process. When we're not deciding to do something, we're deciding not to.

"We've all heard about the woman who wanted to do something—go to medical school, I think. She said, 'Well, I'd do it, but by the time I finished I'd be forty-five years old.' And the answer was, 'How old will you be if you *don't* go?'

"Now on the one hand, that story makes a lot of sense.

But on the other hand, it bothers me a lot. It implies there's no cost to such a decision. But there is. There's always a cost. And before you go out and prepare for anything new, you have to count the cost. There may be times in your life when you have to say, 'It isn't just a question of how old I'll be if I go back to school—or undertake something else—but also of how broke I'll be, how worn out I'll be, how many sunsets I'll miss.' There is always a cost.

"Make no mistake, there are costs to *not* making the choice, too. What I'm saying is, we have to weigh the costs on both sides and then make the best decision we can. Don't give up on yourself. Decide what you want to do. And above all, don't be afraid to dream big but start small."

In our culture we seem to convey that we must be good or great at whatever we do—all or nothing. I know two men who traveled for several days in Mexico on business. They did not know each other before the trip. One was a returned missionary who had served his mission there, the other a professor of Spanish. One day, after the trip, I was talking with the professor and mentioned the missionary Spanish of his fellow traveler. This information was a total surprise to the professor; he thought I must be mistaken. "He spoke not one word of Spanish the whole trip," he said. "I had no idea he could speak Spanish."

My guess is that, in the presence of an expert (the professor), fear kept the amateur (the missionary) from even attempting his rusty language abilities. How sad!

We see this phenomenon often—in the perfectly competent church music director who has a near panic attack when a professional musician joins the choir, in the church speaker who becomes extremely nervous because higher authorities are present, in the employee fearful of even writing a memo to a colleague who is known as a better writer.

The day of the amateur is dead. But it can be resurrected. When you identify what your love is, go for it. If not in a big way, as a volunteer, a part-timer, an amateur. Keep your hand in it, enjoy it, and grow from it. Make your own happiness and prepare for your own future, to the extent possible. Dream and dare.

4

Who Are You?
Who Will You Be?
Defining and Redefining Self

We can plan no journey without first being pretty sure where we are. And we can start no effective process of change without first recognizing to a large extent *who* we are.

I once saw a list compiled by a group of historians of what they felt to be the ten most significant developments or events in the history of the world. Making a similar list for your life can be an interesting experience. Have you ever tried to list the ten most significant events in your past that have made you who you are?

Once you've made this attempt at defining yourself, must you settle for that definition, or is it possible to *rede*-fine, *re*design, *re*-create yourself for the future? The answer is yes, it is possible—you can make changes in yourself.

Now, it's time for another list: a list of the ten events, attitudes, or attributes you would like to see in yourself in the future to make you who you want to become.

The list-making (the defining) is the easy part. Reaching within yourself to wrench out the attitudes and traits you choose to be rid of (the re-defining) will be harder. Change can be painful.

A friend told me of an experience he had in the Samoan Islands. While snorkeling, he watched an old fisherman stalk an octopus. The traditional island fisherman is armed only with a pair of goggles and a thin spear. With skill and cunning, he dives into the relatively shallow waters of the reef and hunts his prey.

On this occasion the wounded octopus nestled into a sort of cave in the coral and held on tight. Since even a small octopus has an enormous grip, finding a way to extricate the creature is a challenge. One method is for the fisherman to offer his arm. As the octopus releases his grip from the walls of his hiding place, one tentacle at a time, to grab the intruding human arm, he can then be brought to the surface.

However, this octopus took his time letting go. Furthermore, the fisherman found it impossible to break free, once the first two or three tentacles were on his arm. My friend, the observer, is a strong swimmer, yet he had to come to the surface for air not only once but twice before the fisherman finally brought up the creature.

So it can be with the many-tentacled monsters within ourselves that we want to be free of. Their grip on us can be awfully strong. We will not always rid ourselves of them easily. But we can eventually free ourselves if we hold out long enough.

In these stories, people face questions of definition and redefinition with varying degrees of success.

This Is Me

If she hadn't been a volunteer at the Oak View Rest Home, Sue might not have discovered how strongly people cling to identity markers or to other means of defining themselves.

She first noticed it with old Mr. Cahill. He was a kindly gentleman, now very old, suffering from emphysema, and not usually coherent. But about a week ago when Sue came to visit with him and feed him his supper he started talking. He didn't actually converse, but just repeated four phrases over and over, in his breathless way: "Born with the century, worked as aide to Harding in the White House, interviewed Lindbergh, given award by Hoover."

Sue tried to ask about each of these, but Mr. Cahill either didn't understand her questions or didn't have the breath to respond. Yet, throughout the meal, he would occasionally repeat the phrases again. Sue knew Mr. Cahill was living in the past as he often did, but today it struck her that there was more to it—that he was somehow establishing who he was through the four events mentioned.

The next evening, Sue was talking to Mrs. Agnes Yountz in the sitting room. This woman was a favorite of Sue's. A bright-eyed, strong-willed, young-at-heart seventy-year-old, Agnes had more energy than most people half her age. Being confined to a wheelchair didn't slow her down a bit, and she constantly moved around the facility, talking with and helping other residents. Several times before, Sue had asked Agnes to talk about her fascinating life as a wife, mother, ski instructor, and small-plane pilot.

Maybe it was because of her observations of Mr. Cahill the night before, but this time Sue noticed things in Agnes's story that received extra emphasis: ". . . soloed at fourteen years of age . . . taught Senator McNeal to ski . . . drove the first school bus route in the Sawtooth Valley . . . never missed a day, even in the big winter of '48 . . . never lost a bus, or a student . . ."

Sue realized that these were the important identity markers in Mrs. Yountz's life. Take these events away and you'd have a different person.

The next day at her work as a university employment interviewer, Sue was still thinking about her observations at the rest home. She wondered if it was only in old people, now looking back over their lives, that the need to establish identities came out so clearly. She decided to find out.

Her first interviewee was a young woman seeking a management position. After the usual questions, Sue asked, "If you were to tell me who you are, without referring to job qualifications, personal traits, or education, what would you say? As far as you can identify, what, in your life, has made you who you are?"

The young woman stammered a bit, then said, "Well, that's a tough question. I'd say I'm a hard worker. Oh, I guess that's a trait. Uh, I'm . . . I've traveled a lot, lived in Europe and Australia. Travel is one thing that's important to me."

She paused a moment, thinking hard, then went on. "I worked in my later teen years as a hotline volunteer for troubled youth. I loved that. It made me feel useful. Uh, I don't know if this is important—I guess it is to me—I was a runner-up in my city's Junior Miss contest. Maybe it's vain to mention, but the program did a lot for my self-esteem."

As the young woman spoke, Sue's question was answered: Not only for old people are identity markers important. Throughout the rest of the week she asked people the same questions and noticed, in all cases, that they came up with markers important to them.

One of her interviewees was particularly interesting to her. He was a forty-three-year-old man who had a lot of trouble with the question. He kept changing his responses, almost as if ashamed of them. He said, for example, that he'd been the eighth-grade valedictorian in his small town, then immediately said, "Oh, that doesn't matter at this point." He later mentioned an award he had earned at his first professional employment after college. Then he said, "I don't know if it meant much—and it probably has nothing to do with this job."

Sue concluded the man was perhaps at a point in life where old markers were less important than they had been previously, leaving him sort of rootless. She sensed he was in the so-called midlife crisis, and suddenly Sue came up with a new definition for that phenomenon: a loss of old identity markers without the immediate establishment of new ones.

Who are you? It's a hard question. "My name is . . ." "I'm from . . ." "I'm married to . . ." "I'm a tax accountant . . ." Nope, these are too simple. They don't really tell who you are.

When pressed further, you may say things like: "A convert to the Church . . . parent of four great kids, one of whom was killed in a hunting accident four years ago . . . I do a little woodcarving as a hobby, and I've won a couple of awards for it . . . I have asthma . . ." These are more meaningful descriptions of the things from which you take your identity—the events, desires, and interests that make you who you are.

When was the last time you thought about your identity markers? If you've lived very many years, you, like the forty-three-year-old in the story, have probably found that some of those markers have changed or are changing. The importance of having won the blue ribbon for the biggest watermelon at the county fair, in your youth, fades with the passage of time. The near-miss car wreck of last year may have become much more of a force in your life.

Some markers are subtle and hard for us to recognize. A

person may think of himself as a hard worker, yet not recognize his deeper need to be *seen* by others as a hard worker. People are seldom simple.

Perhaps the most important question about identity markers is whether they can be consciously changed and updated. Growth and change require us to establish new markers as we go through life. If not, we may end up like Mr. Cahill, living on memories. Not that memories are bad, but it seems unfortunate when a person is "stopped" at *any* age from growing and changing.

Looked at positively, the "midlife crisis" may be a healthy growth experience. Not necessarily an untying of all the old knots and an escape to a life of irresponsibility— as the term is popularly construed—a midlife crisis might be better thought of as a series of midlife junctures or decision points.

Escape negates the first half of one's life. How much better it is to consider midlife questions as opportunities to redefine self and to search out new and better purposes for living.

Write It Down

The mission field was on Cody's mind lately. It had started a few months ago as Jared, his oldest boy, got closer to the age of nineteen and began to anticipate serving a mission. Then today's surprise visit from Tim—Elder Cohen—an old missionary companion, like a ghost from twenty-three years ago, had prompted him even more to think back on days now so hazy and blurred and remote as to be almost a dream. Tonight, with most of the family involved with other things, he sat with his missionary journal on his lap, starting a systematic review — something he had never done in all the years since his mission.

A few hours later he had covered a lot of ground: his first thirteen months in Denmark. Four transfers, five companions (two he loved, one he couldn't stand, and two he found okay), bouts of homesickness, several baptisms, a couple of near miraculous healings, a small auto accident, quite a number of tremendously "high" days, a few real "lows," a sort of semi-"Dear John," and even a new mission president.

The review was a fascinating experience. He remembered clearly, for example, the negative feelings he'd had for his third companion, and wondered now, with several years' hindsight, how much of the problem was his own. He remembered as clearly as if it were yesterday the night he baptized Sister Koralewski, the first convert he had helped to teach.

Other entries were surprising to him. For the life of him he couldn't remember certain people and events written about in detail: a drunk who followed them home; a dinner at the mission home when the power went off and they had to light candles; a branch Christmas program where he played the part of an offstage angel announcing the birth of Christ; discussions in people's homes where odd things happened, such as the family dog licking his shoe throughout the lesson presentation. Reading about some of these events was like reading about the life of a stranger.

Other things were quite puzzling to him: why his attitude toward a couple of other religious groups was so negative (why had he seen them as competitors?); who a certain Mrs. Bolle was, who fed them regularly, darned his socks, and lectured him on being too serious (shouldn't he remember someone he had spent so much time with?); how some families being taught suddenly disappeared from the journal (what had happened to them?); how he could be, at times, so immature in his biases and views and on the same page state deep feelings and ideas that could pass for his own even today.

Besides enjoying a review of the facts, Cody had come to a few interesting insights. One was how the realities described in the journal didn't often match the distillations of memories filtered through the years. In a few cases he was humbled to see how badly his memory had distorted reality. He was not assigned as a district leader as soon as he had thought he was, for instance. In other cases the journal indicated that he did pretty well at things he thought he had failed at. His description of the difficult time with his third companion, for example, revealed that he had tried harder to make things work out than he'd remembered.

Cody was glad to see, too, that on his third day he had written, "Had a good cry last night in bed." Maybe it was an odd thing to be glad to read. He had remembered the event well, yet would have predicted that his young machismo wouldn't have let him write it down at the time. But there it was, as honest as could be.

With a jolt, Cody realized that his biggest mistake in the field of journals was stopping regular journal writing after his mission. Well, maybe it was time to start again.

Cody is blessed to have a record of this key part of his life. Imperfect though it is, still his journal is certain to be more accurate than his memory, especially after twenty-three years. Even more important than accuracy of facts is accuracy of feelings.

Cody is fortunate not only to have a journal of his mission but also that the record is apparently honest and written for him—not for an imagined future audience. We often hear the admonition to write a journal or life history for the benefit of our children and grandchildren. This *is* one purpose of such writing. But if it becomes the main focus, great distortion can occur. A journal is not a letter home. Forget whether someone else might read it. If you write for an audience, you will "color" your life considerably and possibly destroy the integrity and humanity of the writing. Ironically, this will greatly lessen its value to future readers.

A particularly bad case of distorting a journal and thereby reducing its value is in the report of a daughter typing her deceased mother's life story for the descendants. In one place the mother had written how angry and upset she was about some event in her life. The daughter refused to type the line, saying, "Mother *wouldn't* have felt that way!"

Few things do more to help us define ourselves and keep track of where we are and where we're going than the regular keeping of a journal. If you're one who hasn't yet started, it's never too late. But don't delay: every day you fail to record is partially or wholly lost forever.

Live by Clichés, Die by Clichés

"I'll be okay in a minute," Maureen said to herself. What worried her was that she had said the same thing ten minutes earlier and ten minutes before that, but she still hadn't been able to bring herself to move. Maureen sat at the dining room table, her chin resting in her hands. She sighed again and looked at the clock on the wall. "Three-thirty. Don will be home in less than two hours. I can't let him see me just sitting here. I'll have to get this stuff cleaned up." Still she didn't move, other than to slowly survey the table full of chores before her. Just looking at it made her tired.

There was a big stack of genealogy papers she had been going to sort and organize way last summer for the family. She'd put off starting them because she wanted to spend real quality time on the project. "Something worth doing is worth doing right," she said to herself.

There were three piles of student papers to grade by Monday morning, if they were to be returned before Christmas break. Never, in thirty years of teaching, had she been this far behind in her paper grading.

There were the boxes of Christmas cards yet to be addressed. Here it was December 16 already, and she'd not yet sent one card. Always before, Maureen had prided herself on having all her cards sent by the first week of the month, even though she thought the whole routine was a useless social custom.

And as for Christmas shopping, well, there was still one more Saturday, but how would she ever get packages mailed in time to her grandkids?

She'd been going to get so much done today, too. But after choir practice this morning, which she'd dragged herself out of bed to attend, she hadn't felt like doing anything. It wasn't like her—it wasn't like her *old* self, anyway. Lately, though, she just didn't know what the problem was.

Her eyes fell on the Relief Society files she'd volunteered to organize, the monthly ward paper she had to type, tomorrow's Sunday School lesson to prepare. She felt like she had too much to do, but she'd always believed a good Latter-day Saint should never turn down a calling.

There was the volunteer work on the county fair committee she probably shouldn't have taken on, but a good friend had asked—and besides, she'd always heard that if you wanted something done, you should give the job to a busy person.

And on top of it all, she hadn't even thought about dinner, which Don had a right to expect in a couple of hours.

She sighed again.

A few minutes passed, and Maureen pushed aside an

urge to sweep everything before her into a heap on the floor. "I've got to get hold of myself," she said. "Okay, deep breaths, Maureen, let's go, you can do it. I'll talk myself into it like I always do."

She leaned back in her chair and started her litany aloud:

"When the going gets tough, the tough get going."

"Nobody ever died from hard work."

"Great people are ordinary people with extraordinary determination."

She recited these mottos again and again, but this time they didn't work. When Don came home near five-thirty, he found her still sitting at the table, staring out of the window.

Maureen has a problem. While we don't know the full extent of it or its root causes, it's clear she has lost track of who she is. Part of Maureen's difficulty may be that she has lived too long on clichés and motivational sayings: "Something worth doing is worth doing right." "A good Latter-day Saint would never turn down a calling." "If you want something done, give the job to a busy person." These and the other sayings she uses to guide her life have value, no doubt. But like all guidelines, they cannot cover all situations.

While these sayings Maureen cherishes may have been distilled from someone's life philosophy, they are not in themselves a philosophy, and they aren't sufficient to produce satisfaction and happiness in and of themselves.

The fact that Maureen has to quote her motivational sayings like a mantra indicates she has relied too heavily on them, rather than developing her own philosophy. Therefore, in a case like this, where she faces a crisis— where, if you will, "the going gets tough"—Maureen isn't "tough" enough to get herself going. And all the repeating of now-empty clichés won't help. When the going gets tough, clichés fail!

Maureen is stressed out, and while she may be right that "nobody ever died from hard work," people *can* die of stress and its related symptoms.

Maureen needs help. Let's hope that when Don gets home, he obtains it for her, rather than providing her another cliché, like "Hey, everybody has a bad day; you'll feel better tomorrow."

Even the most meaningful motivational proverb becomes shallow and useless if it isn't internalized. Maureen performs for others: her family, her students, society, friends—all worthy recipients, to be sure. But what about Maureen? What does she do that *she* wants to do? What are *her* priorities? A life without priorities will likely be eaten up by the plans and goals of others, leaving us without fulfillment of our own stewardship and without a proper definition of self.

Adjusting Can Hurt

"Everybody get what they needed?" Gary asked, as the three came out of the convenience store.

"Yep," TJ said.

"More than I needed," Fred grunted. Gary didn't know what that meant, but figured he'd find out soon enough. The three of them had stopped for gas, pop, candy bars, and night crawlers. It was a beautiful spring morning, and three generations were going fishing: Grandpa Fred, son-in-law Gary, and Gary's 16-year-old son, TJ.

"Want to drive awhile, TJ?" Gary asked, knowing what the answer would be from one who so recently had obtained his license.

"I could probably stand it," TJ said, with his usual understatement. He grinned and hurried around to the driver's side of the pickup.

"Do you want the middle or the window, Grandpa?" Gary asked.

"Don't care," Fred answered sullenly as he slid into the middle position on the truck seat. Gary and TJ looked at each other and TJ pulled onto the highway leading up the canyon.

After a moment's silence TJ asked, "What happened in there, Grandpa?"

"Aw," Fred snorted, "I'm just an old man and don't want nobody to notice it, I guess. I've never been old before, and I'm still learning."

"Oh, you're not old, Grandpa," TJ said.

"Like a pig isn't pork," Fred said with a chuckling sound that was without mirth. "Only seventy-nine. I suppose it's time I admitted to a bit of age. They say it takes about ten years to get used to how old you are!"

"I hope I'm still fishing at seventy-nine," Gary said.

"There's those that think I'm too old already to go on these jaunts anymore—like Mama. She'll sit home worryin' till I get back."

TJ asked, "What were you telling that clerk about how she could keep her discount if . . . something?"

"Lost my temper there, TJ. Shouldn't've, but I did."

It was quiet until Fred decided to go on. "You know, I guess I been fighting gettin' old since one night when I was forty-two. I heard a noise out back of the house and went out to see what it was. I seen a group of kids out in the alley behind the tool shed we had at the Camden Street place. As I walked out to see what was goin' on, I recognized a couple of 'em in the moonlight—neighborhood boys. I don't think they was hurtin' anything, chasing a cat or somethin'.

"Anyway, I heard one of 'em say, 'Hey, there's the old man,' and they took off. I couldn't believe it, them thinkin' of me as an old man. And I was only forty-two! I remember I just stood there in the dark and thought about that. Oh, I know I probably said the same thing about forty-two-year-olds when I was a kid, but somehow it really amazed me to have 'em think of me that way. Stupid, huh?

"Mostly it's not getting old that's so bad, it's how people treat you. People treat you different when they think you're not only over the hill but coastin' with no brakes down the far side. You get left out of conversations—like you're not even there. Or people speak louder when they talk to you, like you was deaf.

"Now, this little gal in the store here, I asked her where the bait cooler was, and she actually *took me by the arm* and pointed me down the aisle!"

TJ glanced over at his grandfather, who went on, "See, you don't get it, do you? Because you're young. Well, when's the last time a clerk took *you* by the arm to show you around a store? Maybe when you were three or four years old, but not since. See, that's how they treat old people—like babies."

"Maybe it was just, oh, I don't know—*respect*, Grandpa," TJ said.

"No," Fred said. "It *isn't* respect. I don't care what they *think* it is. It's really that they think you're incompetent. They give you their senior-citizen's discount, and then they treat you like you don't have the sense to count your own change. That's when I started to tell her to keep her discount."

Fred has discovered that some discounts come with a built-in cost. It's interesting that most public facilities give their discounts to two groups only: old people and children. (Incidentally, what Fred is fighting—the feeling that others will see him as less competent — is what many hand-icapped people have to fight throughout their lives.)

Life is filled with transitions, occasions when we rework our definition of who we are. Some transitions are positive, some negative. In our youth we may long for the suppos-edly greater advantages of adulthood and try to hasten its arrival. Therefore, that particular adjustment tends to be a positive one.

Other transitions — like aging — are viewed as less posi-tive in our culture, and the adjustment most people go through during these phases requires a rather major redefi-nition of self. The process can be painful, but if there's one way to lessen the pain, it's to take matters in hand and make the necessary mental adjustment.

Roads Taken, Roads Not Taken

Terry Glazier relaxed until the commercial ended, then leaned forward in his seat to be close enough to the large microphone. He was in the middle of being interviewed live by Dean Skyler, talk-show host, about his latest novel. Interviews weren't something Terry enjoyed a lot — he'd rather write than talk about writing — but he was getting used to them, since his agent told him he'd better if his book was to succeed.

"We're back," Dean said. "This is Dean Skyler visiting today with Terry Glazier, author of *Forward, March*, a new Bantam novel. Terry, we've talked about some of your pre-vious work. Now I want to ask you, what's the greatest honor or reward or compliment you've had or aspired to?"

"A good question, Dean," Terry said. "I suppose you mean what's the greatest honor I could aspire to for my work, my writing. And I guess that would have to be the Nobel prize for literature. But I'd settle for a Pulitzer." He laughed, a little uncomfortable with a question about awards unlikely ever to be his.

"But, you know, the first thing I thought of when you asked me about honors is how we seldom get complimented on the things we value most. My dad, for instance, was a successful trial attorney, but I think what he wanted to accomplish more than anything else was to develop new strains of roses. He'd win a big case, and the thing he'd worry about was whether he had to start working on a new one before the next flower show or contest.

"Maybe it's only the 'grass-is-always-greener' syndrome, but in my own case, you know what I'd really like most to be? A guitarist, a jazz guitarist—a great one. I mean, you can give me the Nobel prize if you want to, but if you want me to be *really* thrilled, give me the fingers and the abilities of a jazz guitarist."

Dean said, "I always wanted to be a great singer, myself, so I know what you're saying. Can hardly carry a tune, but still . . ."

Terry went on, "Of course, I don't know how often our *interests* match our *abilities*. In my own case, what if I'd set out to be a guitarist—would I have made it?

"I wonder a lot, both as a writer and as an observer of people, just how often roles and people match up. I mean, is Lech Walesa, the Polish Solidarity leader, a better electrician or political leader? What if he'd never gotten involved in union affairs? Would Poland—or the whole eastern bloc, for that matter—have moved toward elections and free travel the way they have?

"The really interesting question is whether there are other electricians, let's say, or teachers, or even prune pickers who could have done as much as he did, but didn't— because they didn't know they could, lived in the wrong era, or read the wrong newspaper. Maybe they just plain didn't try.

"It's like saying Miss America is the most beautiful and

talented young woman in the country. Can we really say that? Don't we have to qualify it by saying she's the most beautiful and talented young woman in the country *who entered the competition?* There could be a big difference!

"Roles and people don't always match up. On occasion, for example, a person with a high aptitude for compassion and service becomes a country doctor, and we say he or she was perfect for it. But probably more often than not, he or she sells real estate or cuts hair or something—where the level of compassion and service aren't so apparent or necessary.

"Some secretary out here in the lobby of this radio station right now might have the aptitude for being the greatest something . . . I don't know, uh . . . trapeze artist of our time—and doesn't know it, doesn't have the slightest clue, isn't even interested. Maybe she's never even been to the circus!

"I find it fascinating that maybe my neighbor, say, who's a plumbing contractor, could have been a great general in some war that—thank heaven—never happened at the 'right' time, with him in the 'right' place. Or it could be that my mailman might have been more esteemed in the world of art than Picasso, but he never picked up a brush."

The roads we take define who we are. But with every road taken, how many other roads are passed by? Do our non-choices define us as much as our choices do?

No one can take all possible roads, not in a hundred lifetimes. Life is precious in part because it is finite and limited, which should cause us to choose wisely how we will spend it.

The central question is: Do we let outside events define us or do we define ourselves? As much as possible, we must opt for the latter.

How many of us let our self-definitions limit us and

keep us from trying some of the things we'd secretly like to do, keep us from even "entering the competition"? Which is better—to enjoy the square dance or to spend a lifetime watching, for fear that someone might notice we're not very good at the do-si-do?

We can't take all roads. All we can do is choose carefully the roads we do take. Are you on the road you want to be on? If not, is there any reason you can't still start on it?

5

*Clearing
the Clutter*

As we begin moving toward being the kind of person we want to be, we must clear away much of the clutter that has accumulated over the years. It's as necessary as clearing away the weeds and old growth in a garden spot in the spring. Unless we do so, new growth can't flourish.

As the years go by, we become covered in scar tissue from life's battles. We learn reactions and behaviors that aren't appropriate or useful. Habits are gained that get in the way of growth. Routine replaces spontaneity; boredom replaces joy in new experiences. Fears keep us from trying new things. Thinking patterns become solidified, opinions calcified. Relationships grow stale and predictable. Cares and concerns wear us down. Responsibilities become burdens; commitments seem like chains.

But none of this has to be! These changes come from our own attitudes—and attitudes can be changed. It's time to reassess our lives and clear out the clutter!

However, in the clearing process we must be careful. As with a new garden, it's sometimes easy to kill *everything*, even the tender young plants, in our zeal for starting over. The right tool for garden clearing is not a flame thrower. We're preparing a spot for living things, not leaving behind a scorched earth.

Yet some have abandoned families, jobs, and responsibilities in an effort to set a new course. Relationships can be revitalized, fears overcome. Bad habits can be replaced with better ones. We can forgive ourselves for past mistakes.

Better one step at a time than too many wild leaps into the unknown.

Happiness depends, to a large extent, on our taking time to clear the clutter. If you're ready to start the clearing process in your own life, the following vignettes may help.

Can I Ever Forgive Myself?

"I talked my son out of a mission," Sister Carter said. The statement seemed to come out of the blue, leaving the startled home teachers with no immediate comment. But there was no time for comment anyway, because the elderly widow went right on talking. "That's what your lesson should have been about today—how I hurt my son by talking him out of a mission."

Brother Jensen thought he realized now what had triggered this response. The home teaching lesson today had dealt with something unrelated, but afterward Sister Carter asked Brother Jensen how his daughter was doing on her mission. They chatted about her for a few moments, then had a prayer together. Brother Jensen and young Cory Ash, a new, fourteen-year-old home teacher on his first visit ever, stood to leave. Sister Carter followed the two of them to the door, where the woman suddenly made her surprising statement. Now Brother Jensen and Brother Ash stood awkwardly in the doorway—half in, half out—while the story poured out.

"He had a scholarship and I thought he ought to stay in school. The thing is, he really wanted to go on a mission. I just didn't think it was as important at the time."

Sister Carter lifted her eyes and peered through the screen door at the snow swirling around the eaves, but her eyes didn't focus on anything, except possibly a scene from the past. "I didn't think much of it until he married out of the Church," she said. "A fine girl, of course . . ."

"I'm sure you did what you thought best at the time," Brother Jensen said lamely.

"I've thought about that mistake every day for thirty years." The woman turned her eyes to young Cory Ash. "You," she said, raising a thin finger at him, "you be sure to go. Don't let anybody talk you out of it."

Thirty years is a long time to carry a burden of self-reproach. By now it's no longer a question of why or how it happened, or of who was to blame. It's just time to forgive.

What if the situation were reversed? What if the *son* had been the one to decide against a mission? Would his mother still hold it against him thirty years later? Or would she have long since decided to let his decision stand and help him get on with his life?

Would she want him to think of that mistake "every day for thirty years"? Or would she hope he could put mistakes behind him by now—as we must all do if we're to progress?

It seems likely she would want her son to get on with life. Why is it so much harder for her to forgive herself? Forgiveness of others is a great thing, but forgiveness of self is at least as important. It's one of the best ways of clearing the clutter.

Maybe Brother Jensen and Brother Ash already know the subject for next month's home teaching lesson.

The Type E Type

The night was warm and quiet, and Colleen sat in the car in the driveway in the dark, hearing the occasional, tiny ticks of the cooling engine. She rested her head back against the headrest and closed her eyes. Tonight's visiting teaching visits had been fine, she supposed, but her heart wasn't in them, she thought guiltily. Why don't I enjoy the visits more? she wondered.

She didn't really have time to go out tonight, but her companion, Sister Buford, had expected her to go. The two had already been out earlier in the month, but once was never enough for Sister Buford, and Colleen didn't want to stand in the way of her enthusiasm. It was good to have a companion who was interested in doing a good job. She really had no choice except to be supportive.

Still, the sisters they taught didn't have any big problems, and Colleen wondered if they really appreciated having to make time for a second full-blown visit every month. Once in a while might be fine, but Sister Buford wouldn't think of ever missing that second visit.

Now it was late, and Colleen still had to help Kristin with her sewing for class tomorrow. She thought she should get inside. But it felt good to relax for a minute. The day had been long. Weren't they all, lately?

It had been such a busy summer and fall, what with the Coombs reunion she had headed up in August, her several Church callings, her taking on additional violin students as word spread of her abilities as a teacher—not to mention the normal family chores. Rex's new job required more social involvement on her part, or was it just that her many other activities made it seem that way? Rex had told her to slow down and not try to do so much, but she knew she should be grateful for the opportunities.

Maybe it had been a mistake to take the evening class at the community college this semester, yet she felt she must keep progressing and learning. But with canning season, school starting for the kids, the kitchen remodeling project she and Rex had undertaken, her Church callings, and Jill's sudden decision to serve a mission, it sometimes seemed too much. She probably shouldn't have accepted the request to play at the funeral tomorrow. The man who died was in another ward, and she hadn't even known him.

Washed by a sudden wave of guilt, Colleen jerked her head up with a start. "Who am I to be ungrateful for the blessings and opportunities I have?" she asked herself. "I can do what's expected of me. Who do I think I am to sit here feeling sorry for myself? I must go in and help Kristin, then get some studying done for class tomorrow night. Why, there are women who do all I do and have a career outside the home, too—not that I can figure out how they do it all."

As Colleen fumbled with the keys, she momentarily clicked the ignition switch to the "accessories" position, activating the car radio. An interviewer was asking a psychologist about something called the "type E person." Colleen briefly wondered what that meant, but she had no time to listen. She turned off the ignition and hurried to her duties in the house.

Uh-oh! Colleen missed hearing what she badly needs to hear. The radio show she turned off was about her type of person—a classic type E. The "E" stands for Everything.

The term was coined to describe the person who tries to do everything, to accomplish too much, to be all things to all people.

Colleen's guilt over taking a moment to think about her life and its direction is a bad sign. Notice the words she uses when she thinks about herself: "had no choice," "didn't want to stand in the way," "sometimes seemed too much," "Who do I think I am?" Notice the references to *should, must, guilt,* and *expectations.*

Although Colleen asks herself good questions (such as "Why don't I enjoy the visits more?" "Who am I to be ungrateful . . . ?" and "Who do I think I am . . . ?"), she fails to take time to think about the answers. The questions themselves make her feel guilty! The guilt then drives her to get back to her "duties" rather than to analyze her life and make more decisions of her own.

It isn't being busy that's Colleen's problem. As a mother, wife, and dedicated church worker, she will always be busy. And, as she recognizes, there are busier people. But Colleen isn't only busy, she's harried. And that comes because she isn't making her own decisions. She's *driven* to do the things she does—driven either by other people or by guiding principles that have gotten out of control. And she's an unhappy person, with a very cluttered life.

The principles she lives by aren't bad. In fact, they all involve helping and serving others. The trouble is, by not looking at what to leave out, by not taking control, by not learning to live a simpler life, Colleen will end up burned out, and therefore not able to help herself *or* others as well as she might have. Even principles of goodness have their limits in practice.

From her youth, Colleen has felt rewarded and praised for her unselfishness. "She hasn't got a selfish bone in her body," one of her friends says about her. Well, if we could give Colleen a gift, it might be just one, very tiny selfish bone—only big enough to cause her to think about her own life once in a while. If she will do that, she may change to a type C person: a Choice-maker, a person who is able to see to her own growth and still help others, by being in control of her own life.

The Burden of Perfection

Charles thought back on the day's events as he drove home. On the one hand, he felt bad about the spontaneous remark he'd heard someone make to Dan. On the other hand, maybe it would help Dan see the problem he so clearly had.

They'd been in a sales meeting where the sales director had talked about being careful to present accurate information when dealing with customers. On the way out, Dan had said something quite innocent to Charles about how he wasn't sure the meeting pertained to him. It wasn't bragging, it was merely a statement of fact. Just then Glen, a colleague, piped up with, "Must be quite a burden, Dan."

"What is? What do you mean?" Dan asked.

"Perfection."

Dan looked at him, puzzled, and Glen, famous for his sarcasm, went on down the hall. Charles said, "Forget it, Dan. You know how Glen is."

It wasn't a fair comment. Dan *was* a careful presenter and really knew his stuff. It was obvious in many ways, though, that the comment precisely stated a real problem of Dan's—perfectionism. Anybody who knew him could see the signs: tremendous self-created pressure, extreme competition, unrealistically high standards, relentless self-chastisement if he fell short of these standards, a seeming lack of satisfaction even when he did accomplish his goals, a drive to be more than anyone *could* be.

Charles was in his office the next day when Dan came in and asked if he could talk for a few minutes. "Sure," Charles said. Dan shut the door and sat down.

"I need your advice, old buddy," Dan said.

"Okay," Charles said.

"I've been thinking about what Glen said yesterday."

"Oh, that. Well, you know . . . ," Charles began.

"It got me thinking. What do you think, Charles? Am I a perfectionist?"

Charles didn't know what to say. "Well, I . . . uh . . . What do *you* think, Dan?"

"Very clever, Charles," Dan laughed. "You're a salesman at heart. The answer is yes. Of course I am. I want to do a good job. I pride myself on it. I've always been that way. What's wrong with it?" Dan paused, noting the tone his voice had assumed, then went on. "Hey, I'm not after you, Charles. Sorry."

"I know," Charles said. "Well, is there a downside to this trait?"

"That's what I've been wondering," Dan said. "I feel like everything I've accomplished in life is because of this drive. But when Glen called it a burden, well, that wasn't the first time I'd realized there are a lot of negatives to it.

"For sure, I feel dissatisfied a lot. I set a high goal, like in sales volume, and I reach it, then I feel like it wasn't enough, you know? I put pressure on myself and then I beat myself up thinking I should have done more. It's really bad sometimes.

"And if I *don't* make my goal, it's even worse. Then it's like I'm a bad person, you know, who isn't worth anything. It's failure of a massive kind, and it really knocks me down for a while."

"Ever feel panic?" Charles asked.

"Why? Does it show?" Dan asked.

"No, but do you? Do you feel panicky in a tough situation?"

"Yes, a lot. When I'm meeting a new client with big potential I sometimes sit in the car outside and feel like I'm really losing it, like I can't go in. I guess everybody gets nervous in new situations."

"Not that way, Dan," Charles said. "The reason I asked about the panic is that I read an article that said perfectionistic people commonly feel this kind of terror when faced with any chance of failure. It also said that, while perfectionists think their high standards cause their success, they actually often achieve less than others, because they're so fearful of failure."

Perfectionism isn't only a burden, it's an impossible and unnecessary burden. The irony for the perfectionist is that in spite of his accomplishments, he is never happy. *Satisfied perfectionist* is an oxymoron.

Perfectionists see their self-worth as tied to their accomplishments. So, instead of rejoicing at accomplishment, perfectionists do what Dan does: when they reach their goal they feel it must not have been a high enough one! And when they don't reach a goal they feel worthless! It's a classic lose/lose situation.

It's all or nothing for them—nothing less than perfection is any good. And since nothing in life is actually perfect, these people often live deeply frustrating lives. Depression is sometimes the result, because perfectionists eventually come to realize that, in spite of their efforts and accomplishments, they are not happy.

Perfectionists operate out of fear. Their fear of failure is so great that risk is often out of the question. They won't try anything where success isn't guaranteed—thereby reducing the potential number of achievements they so desperately want.

The difference between perfectionism and striving for excellence is like the difference between the Grand Canyon and an irrigation ditch. Perfectionists often say they are only striving for the best and ask, as Dan does, "What's wrong with it?" Well, in the case of perfectionists, there's plenty wrong: their self-esteem is misplaced, they can't accept "good"—only "best"—their striving comes out of fear, and they never attain satisfaction.

Perfectionists can help themselves by thinking hard about whether the things they work so hard at really matter. Often they find that the things they give so much effort to bring them little satisfaction, after all. Such attitude adjustments are the beginning of a "cure" for perfectionism.

Habits, Good and Bad

A few weeks back, Ken and Laura Ewell decided to work together on habits each of them wanted to change. Ken chose to work on overeating and excessive snacking, and Laura on her lack of interest in exercising. With support from each other they got off to a pretty good start. Now let's look in on them, on day twenty-one.

It's about seven-thirty in the evening, and Jason, the Ewells' seventeen-year-old son, has come home from his job at the pizza parlor, bringing with him a pizza that hadn't been picked up. Laura walks into the kitchen in time to hear Ken saying to Jason, "Oh, boy! Pineapple, pepperoni, mushrooms—the works! And still warm? All right! Let me at it."

"I thought you were on a diet, Dad," Jason says.

"Well, what am I supposed to do when you tempt me like this?" Ken answers good-naturedly. "You guys would sit here and eat in front of me? Besides, I've been good for three weeks. And it isn't really a diet. And we're only talking one slice. And . . ."

Laura raises her eyebrows. "Now, Ken, you can do what you want, but you asked me to be your conscience, so I'm reminding you it's only been an hour since dinner—at which you got plenty of nourishment—and this pizza constitutes calories you really don't need."

"Get thee behind me, conscience," Ken laughs, as he takes a slice of pizza. "You don't meet up with pineapple, pepperoni, and mushrooms every day."

An hour and a half later, Ken finds Laura reading a magazine. "Ready?" he asks.

"Oh, is it time?" she says.

"Same time as always," Ken answers.

"I don't know," Laura says. "I hate to go out when it's so cold."

"Hey, what's this? Now I have to be the conscience. You said for me to drag you out jogging even when you didn't want to," Ken says. "What's it going to be?"

"I can miss once, can't I? Maybe I actually hate jogging."

"Hey, don't ask me. All I know is, once I miss it's easier to miss again. But, as you observed with the pizza, I'm no example. What the heck, maybe I won't go tonight, either." He starts for the kitchen to see if there is any pizza left.

An undertaking to rid ourselves of a bad habit sometimes appears to be a small task, but it seldom turns out that way. Ken and Laura's good intentions are being undermined, and they may soon find themselves back where they started. Let's look at a few habit principles.

First, Ken and Laura are wise to work *together* on

changing their habits. Support is necessary and helpful. Their reminders to each other are good. But when personal commitment is weak the outside "conscience" may have little effect. Enlist the help of others, and commit to them that you *will* listen when they try to help.

Second, it's important to replace old habits with new ones. Ken needs something to substitute for snacking. Laura needs an exercise she likes better than jogging in the cold. Since habits provide a certain measure of pleasure and comfort (if not, we wouldn't continue them), the substitute must provide similar satisfaction. If Laura actually hates jogging, as she says, her chances of success at this form of exercise are minimal. Better to find something she enjoys more. Willpower can only push us so far, and in the long run it's a poor substitute for desire and enjoyment.

Third, temptations will come and should be planned on. Ken needs a system for dealing with the tempting snacks he will see others eating. Usually the strongest urge to resume a habit passes in *three to ten minutes.* By holding out for that long, even if it means locking himself in the bathroom, Ken will have won most of the battle. (This is assuming he is not actually, nutritionally hungry; real hunger won't go away. But the emotional craving for a snack will —when there's a plan and a substitute.)

Fourth, eighty percent of people attempting to change habits have relapses within three months. These usually occur when the worst is past and their guard is down. Many bad habits, such as smoking, come from emotional distress, and the majority of people who relapse do so when they are emotionally distressed—bored, angry, anxious, depressed, lonely.

Fifth, unfortunately, many people see a lapse as a relapse. When Ken had one piece of pizza, he could have stopped there. But by skipping his exercise and going for even more pizza, he is exhibiting behavior that puts him in danger of losing all he's gained—or, in this case, of gaining all he's lost—in the last three weeks. A dented fender isn't a totaled car! Eating one forbidden doughnut doesn't justify finishing the bag!

Sixth, new habits take time. Plan on three weeks to acquire a simple behavior like consistently remembering to brush your teeth after lunch.

Finally, goals must be realistic. Sometimes people take on too much and set goals that are too far down the road to be motivating. Perhaps Ken could have the occasional piece of pizza if he remains strong about refusing the mid-morning sweet rolls at the office.

In clearing away the clutter of bad habits, be tough. But be realistic, too, and leave room for exceptions. The dieter who won't eat a bite of cake at his surprise birthday party ruins the party for everyone.

What Bothers You and Why?

A young sister missionary sits across the desk from her branch president at the Provo Missionary Training Center. "And on top of everything else," she says with frustration in her voice, "my companion made my bed for me!"

"Oh, that's good," the president says.

"Good? *I* didn't think it was good!"

"You didn't?" the president asks.

"Certainly not," the sister says. "I'm old enough to make my own bed."

"Is that why you think she did it?" the president asks, incredulous. "Because she thinks you aren't old enough to make your own bed?"

"Well, she must think I can't take care of myself."

Two women, close friends, were talking. One said, "You know, I doubt I've ever said this to anyone—even you—but I think the real reason I've never married is that I can be interested in a guy, and then, as soon as he shows any interest in me, I start to wonder what's wrong with him."

"What? I don't get it," the second woman said.

"No, you wouldn't, because you feel okay about yourself. What I'm saying is like what Groucho Marx or somebody is supposed to have said—something like, 'I wouldn't want to join a club that would want me for a member.' That's how it is with me. I assume there's something wrong with any guy who develops an interest in me. Otherwise he wouldn't be interested."

A man had gone to the personnel office to have a confidential talk with the employee-relations counselor. His concern was with his immediate supervisor. "I really don't think it's because she's a woman. I think I'm modern or liberated or mature enough to handle that just fine. I had a female supervisor once before, and I got along well with her. But this one—whew!—she's something else."

The counselor asked, "What would you say is the problem? How does she come across to you?"

"Preachy. Preachy and bossy. It's kind of subtle, but there's a sermon in everything she says—like she's talking down to me."

"Do you think others notice? Does it bother other people in your section?" the counselor asked.

"No, that's the funny part. I don't think it bothers anyone else. Just me. So maybe it is my problem. But I don't need this woman to preach at me. She's like my mother."

A man was talking with his grown daughter. "I wish," the daughter was saying, "I understood Mom better. I can't *talk* with her. It's like she's not honest or open with her feelings. When we get into anything important, she never gets involved, she backs off, she never reveals herself. It's as though she doesn't care."

"You're right about how she reacts to emotion, but I don't think it has to do with not caring," the father replied. "From what I know of her upbringing, this reaction comes from the fact that her dad made fun of or punished the kids when they cried. He wouldn't tolerate it, called them sissies. I think your mom came to see any kind of emotion as a weakness and learned to keep it all in."

A man comes home with a new car. He feels great, not only about the car but also about his feeling of being a good provider and his decisiveness in making the purchase. "Just like Dad must have felt when he used to do the same thing," he thinks, remembering days long past.

He is, therefore, surprised when his wife is less than excited. She's thinking, "I wonder why he never involves me in these decisions. My father would *never* have made such an expenditure without consulting Mom."

A roommate sees simple kindness as condescension. A woman can't accept how a normal male possibly could be interested in her. A man sees preachiness in behavior where others see normal supervision. A woman sees emotion as weakness. A man feels good about his role as unilateral decision-maker in the family; his wife feels left out.

These are examples of how differently people see the world and how hard it is for us to figure out the motives and thoughts of others—or of ourselves. Why do certain things bother me that don't seem to bother others? Why does one faculty member at a university scream at a student who parks in a faculty space, while a colleague shrugs it off? Why does a child's late arrival for dinner infuriate one mother, while next door another handles it with aplomb?

Some people go around being bothered all day long. They think it's because bad things happen to them with greater frequency than to others. Is this really the case, or is it that other people handle their troubles in a better way?

Most of us like to think of ourselves as rational creatures. But in actuality, many of our behaviors, emotions, assumptions, beliefs, certainties, and ways of handling the world stem from deep in our childhood. Our responses are often automatic and not thought out at all. They feel so right to us—even when they may be built on fallacies and misconceptions about other people and the world—that we *create* "rational" explanations in order to justify what we want to do anyway!

This is not to say that automatic responses are wrong, or less credible than other so-called rational responses. But if we can recognize the fact that many of our emotions and feelings come not from events or environment but from our basic interpretations of events and environment, we can start to figure out why certain things bother us so much. We can then work on changing our outlook and our sometimes-cluttered responses.

Reassessing

It was testimony meeting, and Tom Michaels stood. "I had an experience last week, brothers and sisters, that really made me think. I have a cousin I've been close to all my life, and she and her husband lost a child a couple of months ago to a terrible, lingering illness. I was talking with Sandy and she was saying how hard it is to handle that their boy is gone. Then she said something that really bothered me. She said, 'You know, we hadn't been very faithful with our tithing lately,' and she started crying.

"I admit I didn't handle it well. I nearly hit the ceiling. 'Are you telling me,' I said, 'you think that because you aren't doing everything you might do, the Lord would come down and punish you? Strike down a child?'

" 'I'm sorry,' I told her, 'but I don't buy that doctrine. And I don't think you do either. I think you're just grasping at any explanation to help you feel that things are fair. And,' I said, 'I don't blame you for seeking comfort, but things *aren't* fair. I think you're looking for meaning behind this thing, but you're only going to find guilt, if you're not careful.'

"I went on to tell Sandy I thought the only meaning in tragedy is the meaning we make for ourselves. I don't believe God causes everything that happens to us. He set up a world where these things happen. It's part of free agency. It's how we handle things that matters."

Bad things do happen to good people—and to bad people. Good things also happen to bad people—and to good people. "For he maketh his sun to rise on the evil and on the good, and sendeth rain on the just and on the unjust." (Matt. 5:45.) If we insist on always seeing "fairness" in the events of this life—the good blessed and the wicked punished—we will find only frustration.

Fairness is not a concept found in the scriptures. If we look for it there or in the world around us, we're going to come to feel that God has a lot of explaining to do!

How odd that we often ask "Why me?" when bad things happen to us, but we don't so often when good things happen. It's interesting, too, that we're so certain we can tell what's bad and good in the long run. With our myopic vision, we tend to label as "bad" anything that isn't what we want at the moment.

While positive gifts, such as the Holy Ghost, depend to a large extent on personal righteous desires and actions, evil follows no discernible pattern. Accidents happen, disease strikes, the forces of nature wreak havoc, and wicked people are allowed to use their free agency against innocent people.

Seeing automatic meaning in all of these things is akin to superstition—where connections are seen that don't exist. Some of these connections make as little sense as saying that since someone's grandmother died when the Milton Berle show came on TV, comedy shows cause death. (What about the puppies born down the street at the same time? Did Uncle Miltie cause that, too?)

Our job is to *create* personal meaning and purpose out of our difficulties, not to waste energy in trying to *find* God-given meaning and purpose. Searching the past for reasons why God would allow a bad thing to happen is of limited value. Looking to the present and the future for ways to make meaning out of tragedy is of much more value.

6

Principles of Growth

The scriptures tell us "all these things shall give thee experience, and shall be for thy good" (D&C 122:7). However, I believe this is only true when we do our part to make things good. Tough times can break some people, as well as strengthen others. We must view things in such a way as to make the good happen, not assume it will happen automatically.

There are ways of looking at things that lead to growth, and there are others that do not. When we believe that outside forces control our destiny, we shortchange ourselves. But when we believe we are in control of our lives, we place the burdens for growth and happiness right where they ought to be—on our own shoulders.

Interesting research indicates that some people are born with more confidence in their ability to control their lives than other people are. Fortunately, this isn't the whole story. Such genetic confidence only accounts for about thirty percent of the difference. The other seventy percent of our confidence (our belief in an *internal* locus of control) or lack of confidence (our belief in an *external* locus of control) is *learned*, not inherited. That's good news for those who want to take more control, because it means that what we learn we can unlearn. Like most things in life, control is a decision.

Attorney Louis Nizer was once asked if there was such a thing as luck in his trial work. He said, "Yes, but it only comes in the library at three o'clock in the morning."

The responsibility for your own life really does rest with you. And while the road of responsibility and growth is steeper, it promises to lead us to ever-greater vistas and expanding horizons, guaranteeing that the trip will be well worth the effort.

In the following vignettes, people encounter principles of growth that make a difference for them and their happiness.

Where Is Your *Sacred Place?*

"Well, I'm on my way to court, Mario," Karl Hooker said as he went past Mario Escobar's office doorway.

"May your sentence be light," Mario called.

It was an old joke between the two. But today, Karl took a step back and said, "And when are we going to get you down there? You've got the build for racquetball."

"Oh, I don't know," Mario said, looking up from his desk. "Maybe one of these days."

"You'd like it, and I could teach you all my tricks."

"And who'd take my nap for me?" Mario laughed.

"You wouldn't *need* one if you got the old blood pumping, my friend."

"Probably true, Karl. Well, one of these days—maybe."

"Okay, guy," Karl said, starting on down the hall to the elevator. "Sweet dreams."

Karl's invitation had been given once or twice a year for the five years he and Mario had worked in adjacent offices. And the outcome was always the same: Karl did his noon-hour thing, and Mario continued to do his.

Karl's "thing" was to go down to the company gym to play racquetball nearly every day ("on my way to court" was his phrase), while Mario closed his door, forwarded his calls to the receptionist, and read while he ate his sack lunch. Then he would sit down on the carpet, with his shoes off and tie loosened, to read some more—usually something light, a novel or a magazine. After a few minutes he would become drowsy, lie down on his back with his feet up on the chair, and doze for ten or fifteen minutes. Refreshed, he would read some more or perhaps catch up his journal, plan his weekend, write a letter to his parents, read in the scriptures, or sometimes just sit and think.

He'd often felt a little guilty about being so sedentary on his lunch hour, especially since most others jogged, went to the gym or the pool, or at least took walks or ran errands.

He was sure that if he started doing one or another of these activities, he would have a good time. But somehow, giving up his quiet time didn't appeal to Mario at all. And it wasn't only the nap; as much as he enjoyed that, he knew he could get along without it. Still, there was something special about the daily break from his otherwise hectic schedule and hectic life. And he knew the next time Karl asked him to join him "in court" he would again respond, "And who'd take my nap for me?" Karl would go to his game and come back invigorated, freshly showered and

shampooed, while Mario would find his own kind of invig-
oration and cleansing in the quiet of his office.

Maybe Mario doesn't care much for exercise. Maybe he
dislikes competition. Or maybe the reason he doesn't want
to give up his quiet time is that he not only enjoys it but
needs it.

People need a place and a time—preferably daily—to
get in touch with themselves. This has been referred to as
the *Sacred Place*, meaning the place or time set aside to
gain a reprieve from the demands of daily life. Momentarily
stepping back from the world allows us to reflect, to plan,
to gather strength, to rest, and to recover.

Those who have no regular Sacred Place experience
may eventually talk in terms of burnouts and breakdowns.
Growth requires a certain amount of solitude and reflec-
tion.

We may stand in awe of people in highly demanding
positions like, say, leaders of nations or large organiza-
tions, whose time is tightly scheduled all day long and half
the night. They run from one meeting or appearance to
another and are always expected to be at their best, because their influence is far-reaching and the camera never
blinks.

How do they do it? How do they maintain the pace?

One of their secrets is that they *schedule in* rest and re-
flection time. They don't leave it to chance. Neither should
any of us.

What is done is less important than the fact of having a
regular stepping back from structured activities so the mind
can unflex, roam, and recover. The process could be as
simple as Mario's lunch break. Many use commuting time
in the same way. Others find their reprieve in long baths,
handwork, music, or bird-watching.

Ask a fisherman if he's seeking the sacred when he heads for the stream, and he may give you a strange look. But ask him if he's really after fish—or something else—and he'll likely admit it's often something else, even if he can't say what the something else is.

Forgive Others and Heal Yourself

The Cornabys were new in the neighborhood. "And what brings you to settle here, after all those years in the East?" Sister Paul asked her new neighbors on her first get-acquainted visit.

"We have family close by," Brother Cornaby said, "my brother in Clearview and her brother in Waltersville. I was raised in Clearview."

"And," Sister Cornaby said, "after our daughter was killed—in a plane crash a year and a half ago—we had her new baby for nearly a year. I raised him that first year, from two months to nearly fourteen months."

"Oh," Sister Paul said, unsure whether to comment on the death or on the baby.

"It was wonderful," Sister Cornaby said. "I felt like I still had a part of Judy."

"What about the husband, the boy's father? Was he . . . is he alive?"

"Oh, yes," Sister Cornaby said quickly. "He was working, traveled a lot—that's why we had the baby." Her voice hardened. "But then he remarried. Took that baby away from us. That's the real reason we're here. We couldn't stay there."

Bryan Gillespie was learning about agony of mind. He still couldn't believe what had happened to him: eighteen years old and charged with negligent homicide. In his own mind, a murderer. It had all been so stupid, so quick, so irretrievable. Driving with friends, showing off, loosened up with a couple of beers, taking a dare to see if Dad's old crate could really pin the peg at a hundred and ten. They'd reached eighty-five when his world ended.

It has been less than a week, and he was still in shock. Hardly a waking minute went by without his seeing the whole thing in his mind, over and over again.

All, that is, except for the actual accident, when he'd slid into the car that had the right-of-way. That part he couldn't remember at all. He only remembered waking, still in his seat belt, hurting from a fractured ankle—his only damage—finding that no one in his car was seriously hurt, and feeling glad to be alive—until he realized that someone in the other car was no longer alive. The other driver, a twenty-two-year-old woman, was dead. Absolutely and totally and permanently dead. Because of him. And Bryan knew he would never forgive himself.

The week passed like a dream. Or more like a nightmare—filled with police and hospital and parents trying to console. He went to the funeral—sneaked in, so no one would know. He could never face the family.

Speakers spoke of her kindness, her upcoming college graduation, her enthusiasm for life. Not one speaker said anything about the cause of the accident, nothing to blame his reckless stupidity. He almost wished they had.

He sat on the back row and watched the girl's distraught family—her parents and two younger sisters—and couldn't even cry.

This morning he sat on his bed, still in his pajamas, looking at the wall. Today was a bright, spring morning, a Saturday, but he had no interest in the day. He had no interest in anything. He heard the doorbell, but gave no thought to it. His mother would answer it.

In a few moments his mother came to his door and said quietly, "Bryan, there's someone here to see you."

"I don't want . . ." he started. He stared in horror at the man from the funeral, the father of the woman he had killed. A short, stocky, and muscular man, his jaw was set, but his voice was soft.

"Bryan," he said, "I've come to forgive you. And to help you forgive yourself." He said no more, but walked over, pulled Bryan up from the bed, and locked his strong arms around him.

"He could break me in two," Bryan thought. But the arms weren't hurtful, only supportive. Tears were coming down the man's face, and Bryan's mother stood at the door weeping, too. It took only a moment before Bryan felt his great sorrow begin to find release, and something told him he had made a start toward getting well.

"All I want is justice," Martha had told the reporters outside the courtroom. That night as she lay in bed she realized that she'd been lying to herself. She wanted a lot more than justice—she wanted revenge.

It had been nine years, nine long years, since her son's murder. And her family would never be the same. Her husband had blamed himself and had become embittered to the point that Martha knew it had been the main force leading to the breakup of their marriage. Her older son had quit going to church, vocalizing that if a God could allow a thing like this to happen to an innocent child, he would have nothing to do with such a God. He had replaced church with alcohol.

And she had focused her own life on following the trial, the appeals, and the current retrial of Danny's killer. She had given up her job to attend every session, and she had given up a lot more.

If it would only end, if there could only be a conclusion to it, if they'd finally put this man behind bars or in the gas chamber! But tonight Martha faced the loss of nine years of her life and wondered how many more this child-killer would take from her.

Once a dear friend had tried to help her begin the process of forgiveness. But at the time Martha wasn't ready for any such doctrine. Now she wondered if it was not the only way.

Otherwise, where would she end up? Outside the state prison some midnight, beside a bonfire, carrying a pro-death placard, cheering and sending up party balloons, and pretending to be happy because, inside, a man was breathing his last poisoned breath? Is this what she meant when she said all she wanted was justice?

"Dear Dad," Gerald wrote. "As a kid I once heard of a woman who wrote letters to her dead husband from the time he died until she joined him. It seemed strange to me then. I didn't know I would someday be doing something similar.

"I want to write this the same way I would if you were alive to read it. It's the only way to express how I feel.

"You treated me—all of us—poorly. Maybe we deserved punishment at times, but we didn't deserve ridicule and the psychological torture you put us through. For years I hated you. You knew it. And that made it worse. You tried to 'break me,' to crush my spirit. And I resisted.

"Three years ago, when I was twenty-four, I went out to the cemetery. By then you'd been there for six years. I kicked your tombstone, shouted at it, called you every name you used to call me, then sat down and bawled for two hours—not for you, but for me. It made me feel better for a while.

"I guess that moment also broke a few things loose inside me. I saw a psychologist a few times, and I started to get a few insights. A few months ago I was reading in the scriptures, and I saw the forgiveness verses in a new light. I knew what I had to do, and this letter is an attempt to do it.

"Dad, it has taken me a long time to even see the need for it, but I can now honestly say, I forgive you."

To move from malice to forgiveness might be one of the longest journeys we can undertake. There is no more powerful cancer than hate, and its treatment can be difficult. Giving up a desire for vengeance may seem like severing one of the driving forces in life. We love to hate. Ironically, hatred actually consumes the hater, while often leaving the hated unscathed.

Hate is a great chasm we build to separate ourselves from our enemy. He is there, and we are here, and we want no connection between us. The trouble is, instead of hurting the other person, the chasm surrounds and imprisons *us*, taking away our freedom as we become more and more controlled by our own wrath.

There is only one way out—to build a bridge of forgiveness that lets us cross over. And the only one who can build that bridge is the one who is inside the enclosure— the one doing the hating.

Hate is a powerful, but negative, principle. Gandhi said that if we all live by the dictum of "an eye for an eye," the whole world will be blind. Surely no one was more "seeing" than Christ, yet even on the cross he begged his Father to forgive those who had placed him there.

When we take the giant step of forgiveness we free ourselves to grow, now that we're no longer under the control of the one who wronged us. We can start to be happy again. It's never too late to forgive.

Service Beyond Regular Channels

"Well, what do you think, brethren? Did we do any good?" Bishop Cutler asked. He sat with his counselors in their last bishopric meeting before their release later that morning.

"Well," Brother Coolige said, with his usual light approach, "the building is still standing. And quite a few people are still coming to church pretty regularly."

Brother Dunn's predictably slower and more serious response came next. "All positions are filled at the moment, and people have responded well to what we've asked them to do. What do you think, Bishop? What's been the greatest thing you've seen happen in the ward as bishop?"

"Been thinking about that," Bishop Cutler said, leaning back in his swivel chair. "I suppose it's easy, at a time like this, to look back and get sentimental and forget the frustrations."

"Sounds good to me!" Brother Coolige said.

"In a ward like this," Bishop Cutler went on, "there are so many good people and good things happening. I could go on all day. But you know, what struck me last week as I was thinking about this, is the way so many of our people go beyond their regular assignments."

"There is a lot of that," Brother Dunn agreed.

"And I don't mean only doing an extra-good job at what they do, but doing things that aren't required or even church-related. Why, we have the Jenkinses volunteering to take in that girl with the family problems from the Eighth Ward. There's Toby Thornton going around fixing appliances for the widows. And Rachael and Silvia, going downtown almost every Saturday to help at the homeless shelter. They've taken other girls, when they could make it, but these two have been regulars whether anybody else went or not."

"Silvia's got her dad going with her now, too," Brother Coolige said.

"Sister Gerhard working with Hospice," Brother Dunn added. "A great contribution."

"That's the kind of thing I mean," Bishop Cutler said. "And here she is almost crippled up herself, and holding a regular teaching calling in Primary, too. How about the van-load of elders who loaded up and went up the canyon to help clean up the flooding? That wasn't a church assign-ment. In fact, by the time I heard about it, they'd already left!

"You know, when I was a branch president at the MTC a few years ago, I saw one of the best examples of this. I knew nothing about it until it was done, either. There was an elder who was low on funds. His district of eight or ten elders just took charge. They all contributed and bought him a badly needed new set of scriptures, a suit, shirts, the works—and they did it all anonymously.

"I asked people in the district how the idea got started. They said the district leader came up with it. His district thought he was perfect. 'Why is he so great?' I asked them. 'Oh, he just cares about everybody,' one told me.

"Well, we have to get in to priesthood meeting, breth-ren. But these things are impressive to me. I'm all for filling callings conscientiously, but when someone—and it's usu-ally someone who's already busy and doing well at what they're asked to do—will go beyond the channels, so to speak, and serve—to me, that's what it's all about.

"I'm not very good at it myself. I've always been active, but I've often been guilty of thinking that when I'd fulfilled my basic callings I was finished. I'm afraid it's fairly typical in an organization like ours that asks a lot of its people. It's easy to feel worn out after doing the required."

Service is tied to so many important things: love of others, happiness, good feelings about ourselves, personal growth. Growth in isolation would be rather meaningless. If our growth doesn't lead us to help and serve others, it will ultimately have little value. Life isn't a solo but a chorus.

Bishop Cutler's question, "Did we do any good?" is one we must all ask ourselves. No matter what type of assignment we may have in a church or service organization, we must find ways to do more than the required—to serve from the heart. *Doing* isn't the same as *doing good.*

Treat Each Day as a Gift

Jana Cullen had arranged to interview her grandmother for a school assignment. In tenth-grade English, the major assignment of the term was an autobiography, which had to include an interview with at least one relative. It was an easy choice for Jana to select her grandmother, Mary Ellen Kinkaid, because she was easily the most colorful person Jana knew.

"So, honey, what do you want to know about this old girl?" Mary Ellen asked when they were seated in her living room.

"Everything, Grandma," Jana laughed.

"Be careful what you ask for, honey. You might get it! And you don't have time to hear eighty-seven years' worth."

"All right, Grandma," Jana said. "I'll ask you questions."

"Okay, shoot."

"Well, I'm supposed to get all the facts about your birthdate and stuff, but we can do that later. What I really want to know about is how you get into all these hobbies and interests. How do you get the energy to do so many things?"

"I get the energy *from* doing the things that interest me, honey. Take the banjo. Always wanted to play one, since I was a girl. Never had a chance, never gave it much thought in the busy years, the years of child rearing and so on. But one day, about twenty years back, I said, 'Why not?'

"Your grandpa was still alive, and he thought I was crazy, but I never worried. I figure I was already crazy when he married me! So I called the college, and they put me in touch with a man who ran the bluegrass group. He got me started, and I kept working at it. I finally got to the point that, for the last many years, I've helped teach that group! And I perform with them, generally.

"See? It was easy. I just had to start, that's all."

"So you were sixty-seven then?" Jana asked.

"I guess so, around there. So what? I wasn't dead yet. And it doesn't really *take* energy—it *gives* it."

"I just don't have any friends whose grandma started playing the banjo at sixty-seven, that's all."

"Their loss," Mary Ellen said.

"And what else? What about the bike trip across the state?" Jana asked.

"Long before your time, honey. Oh, that was just a lark. I don't bike anymore. I'm too brittle, they tell me. Now I only swim. Your dad was about your age, and he dared me to cross the state with him. It was a silly conversation, and he had no idea I'd do it. I was about forty-five. You've seen the clippings. Made the papers."

"Yes, and Dad's told me about it lots of times. He says he could outdo you on speed and pumping up the hills, but you could keep going all day long. It about killed him, he says."

"I guess I gave him a run for his money, all right."

"You're amazing, Grandma. I could never do that."

"What, at sixteen? You can do anything you want to do, Jana. At sixteen or forty-five or eighty-seven—with maybe a *few* reservations by that time."

"Well, what's coming up next? Any new projects in the works? I mean, besides the trips you make every year and the normal run of concerts and parties and things you do and books you read."

"You think I'd tell you, so you could get your dad all riled up and have him come over and tell me to 'be careful'? Forget it. Of course I have something cooking. Until they carry me out. You'll find out in time."

"Another question I have to ask for this assignment is about your philosophy. 'What are some guiding principles of your life?' is the question."

"Take each day as it comes, and find a way to enjoy it. No matter how busy you are, take some time and do what you want to do. Otherwise—poof!—your life is gone and all you did was bottle peaches and sweep floors and change diapers.

"Unless there's a cyclone or a flood on its way down the valley, have a good time each day. This thing about smelling the roses—do it. Each day is precious—a gift. If you don't enjoy something in the day it's like somebody gave you a gift and you sent it back unopened.

"That's about it, philosophy-wise, for this old girl. Live while you're alive. Life is too quick not to get all the pleasure you can out of it."

Horace Kallen, a philosopher, said: "There are persons who shape their lives by the fear of death, and persons who shape their lives by the joy of life. The former live dying; the latter die living. Whenever I die, I intend to die living."

There are days that require solid duty, from dawn to dusk— or beyond. But days that don't allow time for enjoyment of nature, friends, music, literature, or art had better be few. Dwight D. Eisenhower said, "Unless each day can be looked back upon by an individual as one in which he has had some fun, some joy, some real satisfaction, that day is a loss." A day is too precious a thing to lose.

What Difference Do You Make in the World?

When the students of Dunfield High School picked up their weekly student newspaper one April morning, they knew instantly something was different about it. For one thing, it was edged in black. For another, the front page consisted of only one long article, with the headline—

Mrs. Angeline Moore: She Made a Difference

The article started like this:

There are no students at Dunfield High who didn't know Mrs. Moore—friendly, loving, demanding, courageous Mrs. Moore, teacher and friend. And now that she's lost the long battle with cancer begun twelve years ago, we can find no student who didn't love and respect her. As students in her journalism class, we dedicate this issue to her.

We don't want to make you weep—we all did that at her funeral last week. We want this issue to be as full of life as she was.

Most of us know her story: She learned at the age of forty-four that she had a slow-acting but terminal cancer. Instead of giving up or going into a panic, she sat down and decided what to do with the last years of her life. She told us often about her desire to make a difference with her life. She said that by knowing her time was limited, she felt she'd been given a gift: the incentive to decide how to focus the remainder of her days. Her family was mostly raised, and she wanted to contribute to society. Her choice was to complete a career goal begun as a college student: to teach school.

She went back to college for the few necessary additional credits, and certified as a high school English teacher. That's when Dunfield High first met Mrs. Moore, for the beginning of ten and a half great years. Her honesty about her illness and her courage in the face of increasing physical difficulties sobered and impressed us, especially since, although she deteriorated rapidly in the last month before her death, she still managed to come to school most days—or parts of most days—until the last week.

Because of her love for the students at Dunfield we asked a number of them to write their comments about her —especially what they learned from her. Here are excerpts from a few of those comments:

"Mrs. Moore was the hardest teacher I ever had. But I think I learned more from her. She made you want to work and do your best. She'd say, 'If you're going to do something, do it right and do it hard, and it will be easier next time.' I tried it, and it worked! It changed me. I didn't do everything I should have, but I did more than I would have." (K.D., Junior)

"I heard she was hard, and I tried to avoid her class. Then my schedule put me into it last year. I thought I would die the first month, but she sat down with me one day after school, and that was that. Once she got hold of you, you had no arguments left. She told me I could slop along through life if I wanted to, but she saw something better in me. 'Stretch,' was the word she kept using. I thought pretty hard about that, and it's made a big change in my outlook." (R.B., Senior)

"Mrs. Moore told me once how she never wanted to hear me say again what used to be my favorite excuse: 'That's just how I am.' She said, 'I don't give a green fig how you *are*. I only care about whether you've got the guts to *become*.' I walked out. Nobody could talk to *me* that way! Then I went home and thought about this woman, and what *she* had become, in the face of her difficulties. I started to see how lazy I'd been. It changed my life, and I told her so on graduation day." (P.C., college student, former Dunfield student)

"I'll never forget how weird I thought Mrs. Moore was, at first. When she started class the first day by just sitting at her desk, I thought she was nuts. When we finally got the message that it was *up to us* if we wanted to learn and that we should be asking questions of her, I learned to like it. When she'd turn back a paper with only a grade and no comments, and expect you to come visit with her to find out why it wasn't an 'A,' that was her way of making us care about doing better. If we didn't care, that was up to us; why should she waste her time writing comments on papers for people who didn't care? Of course, with her style, people soon did care. She'd say, 'If you don't want to do better, don't. But if you want to do better, *ask* people how you can do better. Don't expect them to tell you unless you ask.' I miss this woman. She made a huge difference in how I look at things." (J.K., Senior)

"I can't tell you how much I loved Mrs. Moore. The last time I saw her, in the hospital, she could barely talk—but she squeezed my hand and said, 'Make a difference.'" (M.S., Senior)

Most of us have seen the classic movie *It's a Wonderful Life,* now a Christmas tradition on many TV channels. The movie has an intriguing theme. Clarence, an angel trying to "earn his wings," tries to show despondent George Bailey that he's really had a wonderful life, by making it so he can walk around town seeing what it would be like if he'd never existed.

"You've been given a great gift, George," Clarence says, "to see how things would have been if you'd never been born." George quickly learns that his rather mundane life has had a surprisingly positive effect on many people.

At times we need to step back and ask ourselves a few questions: Am I making a difference? How will the world be different because I'm in it? How will I be remembered? How do I want to be remembered? Am I willing to learn and grow and change?

Getting the answers we want may require changes in the things we do, the way we spend our time, the way we treat people. But, as Mrs. Moore said, "I don't give a green fig how you *are*. I only care about whether you've got the guts to *become.*" We *can* change, we *can* become, we *can* grow.

Mrs. Angeline Moore: She Made a Difference. There are few better obituaries.

It's not too late to make your decision on the contribution you want to make to the world. Your happiness and the happiness of many others may depend on your decision.